BASE COMMUNITIES

Base Communities

An Introduction

**MARGARET
HEBBLETHWAITE**

GEOFFREY
CHAPMAN

Geoffrey Chapman
A Cassell imprint
Villiers House, 41/47 Strand, London WC2N 5JE

First published 1993

British Library Cataloguing-in-Publication Data
A catalogue record for this book is available from the British Library.

Cover photographs by Carlos Reyes

ISBN 0-225-66680-4

Printed and bound in Great Britain by
Mackays of Chatham, plc

Contents

2 Base community is about the basics of Christianity   44

Contents

vii

Acknowledgements

Material first published in *The Tablet* and *Alpha* has been adapted and expanded. The poem on p. 94 is reproduced by permission of the author, who has asked not to be named.

Other extracts are reproduced by permission of their publishers: see Bibliography for details.

Copyright for the extracts remains with the authors and publishers, who should be contacted for permission to make any further use of them.

Introduction

What is a base community? Certainly there is a lot of excitement and interest about this 'new way of being Church', as it is often described. And yet I have known people from the first world to have attended week-long workshops on basic Christian community, only to come away saying 'But I am still very unclear about what exactly a base community *is*'.

It is not easy to say exactly what something is, when you are dealing with a grass-roots, bottom-up development that takes a different shape in every different culture. You cannot point to one and say 'That is what it looks like', because the next one will look different.

Nonetheless we do need to try to answer the question, especially since the term has come to be used in the first world in rather different senses. The understandings range from a way of perking up the parish at one extreme, to a go-it-alone group set against the institution at the other. Meanwhile the theology of base community found in the third-world countries remains surprisingly constant, throughout their variety of forms. It is this underlying theological concept we need to look at, not just a list of examples.

Base communities are associated mostly with Latin America. 'Liberation theology' — the new theology from Latin America that makes an option for the poor — has now become a household word, and one of the best ways of explaining base communities is to say that they are the Church context from which liberation theology has sprung, and to which liberation theology in turn leads.

But base communities are not only Latin American. The development in the Philippines is just as remarkable as that in many Latin American countries, and Africa is pushing forward with great strides too. The Tanzanian theologian Laurenti Magesa wrote in a letter to Joseph Healey:[1] 'Ecclesiologically they are the best thing that has happened since the New Testament.'

Then there is the question of whether base communities can or do exist in the developed world as well as in third-world countries — a difficult and complex question to which I devoted my previous book, *Basic Is Beautiful*.[2] If my examples in this book come almost entirely from the third world, that is not because I think you cannot have a first-world base community. It is rather because I think the third world has worked out what it is talking about, and the first world needs to stop and listen in order to sort out its own muddled thoughts.

Magesa used the term 'ecclesiologically', which may be a long word, but means simply that base communities have to do with the nature of the Church. The usual name used for base communities in Latin America — even by the least educated — is 'basic ecclesial communities'. And so, as this book examines, step by step, precisely what a base community is, it also finds itself examining precisely what the Church is.

So this book falls within the category of ecclesiology, though you do not need to be a theologian to read it. It also comes under pastoral theology, because base communities are all about the process of working with people, especially the most needy. And at the same time it is an anthology, for every point is illustrated with stories, quotations and anecdotes, many of which provide inspiring examples to us. Through them we read the message of hope that the base communities bring to the Church — and that message of hope is badly needed today, at a time when so many people are depressed or disillusioned about the Church.

The book closes with three appendices, which together provide all the background that the ordinary student of the subject needs to be well informed on the matter. There is a glossary of terms from liberation theology, which can be thought of as a bluffer's guide.

[1] July 1983.
[2] HarperCollins, January 1993.

It provides a quick way into a language and a thought system that can be baffling to outsiders until they have cracked the code, as well as a handy reference guide to the date of Medellín or the spelling of Gutiérrez.

Then there is an introduction to Paulo Freire. Everyone who knows anything about base communities knows that they drew on Freire's educational methods, but how many have ever actually read Freire?

Finally there is an appendix of documentation. The Latin American Bishops' conferences at Medellín and Puebla are spoken of over and over again, yet it can be remarkably difficult to lay hands on the documents. Here I reproduce the crucial sections that gave base communities their boost. Rome is usually thought of as the great opponent as far as base communities go, and yet the true position is a lot more nuanced than that. Pope Paul VI and Pope John Paul II have both uttered cautious encouragement for the communities, even if their policies and appointments have seemed to lay more emphasis on caution than on encouragement. Their most developed statements on the subject are given here, in extracts from the Vatican documents *Evangelii Nuntiandi* and *Redemptoris Missio*—both essential reading matter for anyone making a study of the subject.

Because I have structured my treatment around the theological concept rather than around a series of case studies, there may be a risk that base communities are seen as a sort of flawless, timeless construct—a piece of heavenly perfection floated down to earth. But the reality is that base communities have erupted messily and painfully into the world at a precise moment of time, as a result of a particular combination of historical circumstances. (Some details of the historical development are given on pp. 120–5.) Base communities have emerged as another chapter in a long and imperfect history of a pilgrim Church forming and reforming itself.

Nor do they stand still, for they respond to needs and opportunities as they arise. Base communities have already lived through appalling persecutions by oppressive regimes, and responded to heart-breaking misjudgements by many of their own hierarchy. They have been developing for scarcely more than a quarter of a century, and we do not yet know what is to become of them.

Yet already we have the sense that, whatever happens in the future, we are dealing with a beacon of hope of lasting import, with a pointer to a truth that can never be snuffed out. I do indeed suggest that there is a universality about the profound and rich ecclesiology of base community. The vision of the Church they bring is of lasting validity, though the expressions of that vision in particular communities are time-bound and changing. It is the same with any living organism.

A word needs to be said about the term 'base community' itself. My preferred term of reference is 'basic ecclesial community' for two reasons. First, it is the term most commonly used by the Latin Americans themselves. Secondly it helps to avoid a looseness of usage, for in the developed West all sorts of groups are found that call themselves 'base communities', and that draw from the Latin American inspiration, while having quite a different ecclesiological status. Talk of 'base communities' has grown and grown, and the spread of the influence is to be welcomed. Yet the time has now come, I feel, to be a little more precise about what it is we are talking about. Without wishing to pour cold water on different types of groups that share a common inspiration, I am now trying to characterize more accurately the nature of the phenomenon found in the third world, and this is not by any means to suggest that the development cannot grow in first-world soil—far from it—but rather to enable us to identify groups that share the same nature rather than groups that share the same name.

The term 'basic Christian community' is also commonly heard — more commonly than 'basic ecclesial community'. This is partly because people are still hesitant to use a word like 'ecclesial' which they do not properly understand. (It just means 'of the Church'.) But it is also because 'basic ecclesial community' did not become standard in Latin America until Puebla in 1979, by which time the two English terms 'base community' and 'basic Christian community' had become fairly fixed.

In this book I will regard all of the following terms as interchangeable: base community, basic Christian community, BCC, basic ecclesial community,[3] BEC, CEB, ecclesial base community, basic Church community, Church base community, small Christian community,[4] small ecclesial community and small Church community. As a rough rule of thumb, any third-world group called by any of those names comes within the scope of this book, because

---

[3] In Spanish, *comunidad eclesial de base*. In Portuguese (the language of Brazil), *comunidade eclesial de base*. Both are customarily shortened to CEB.

[4] This is the standard term in most of Africa.

I see them as a single phenomenon.[5] First-world groups going by those names[6] may or may not be part of the same phenomenon.

Without further delay now let us board our plane and take a glimpse at what has been happening in Mexico and Brazil, in Malawi and Guatemala and far beyond. And the route we fly in these four chapters will be mapped out — not geographically — but by four different yet interrelated ways of answering the question 'What is a base community?'

[5] Every rule has its exceptions. Sometimes in Asia a base community is distinguished from a basic Christian community by including members who are not Christian. In the Philippines a distinction is sometimes drawn between the more churchy basic ecclesial communities and the less restricted basic Christian communities. But as a rule of thumb the principle holds.

[6] e.g. *comunità di base* in Italy, *comunità ecclesiali di base* in Italy (the two groups are quite different from each other), *base communities* in Holland, *comunidades cristianas populares* or *comunidades cristianas de base* in Spain.

1

Base community is the basic cell of the Church

There is an old and familiar saying that 'The Church has four marks by which we may know her: she is One, she is Holy, she is Catholic, she is Apostolic.' And just as the Church has four marks, so I like to speak also of 'four marks' of basic ecclesial community, which are in fact four senses of 'basic'. (I first developed this idea in a series of articles in *The Tablet* in 1988.) Not surprisingly, the four senses of 'basic' can be roughly matched up with the four marks of the Church—'one, holy, catholic and apostolic'.

Supporting this approach is a Pastoral Document signed by fifteen Mexican bishops and archbishops, which said: 'The basic ecclesial communities assume the point of view of the poor and thus affirm with new depth the essential themes of the Church: one, holy, catholic, and apostolic.'[1]

First, then, *the Church is one*; and *the basic ecclesial community is the basic cell of the Church*. That is, it is not a breakaway Church, it does not exist in isolation, it is in communion with the rest of the body, making a single unity.

Secondly, *the Church is holy*; and *the basic ecclesial community is about the basics of Christianity*. That is, it gets back to what the

[1] 'The Base Ecclesial Communities, Church in Movement', signed at Guadalajara, Jalisco, 7 April 1989, 3.5.

whole Christian business is basically about, which is holiness, discovered through such qualities as love and sacrifice and mission, stripping off the accumulated clutter of centuries and returning to a truly scriptural faith.

Thirdly, *the Church is catholic, which means universal*; and *the basic ecclesial community is about the base of society*. That is, it has an option for the poor, so that there is no discrimination on grounds of race or income, of education or cultural background. What is more, the poor are not included just to be people at the bottom, in the same way that they are at the bottom in society, but they are brought up to the front, so that they can teach everyone else.

Fourthly, *the Church is apostolic*; and *the basic ecclesial community is about the base of the Church*. That is, it lives out the well-accepted but rarely implemented principle of the apostolate of the laity, in which all members of the Church, not only the ordained, have a ministry to exercise in the spreading of the gospel.

These chapters will develop each of these four 'marks', under a number of different principles. Each principle will be briefly explained, and then it will be illustrated by one or more passages from a wide variety of third-world sources, each of which not only tells a story but also demonstrates an ecclesiological point.

BASE COMMUNITY IS SMALL

If the basic ecclesial community is the basic cell of the Church, then obviously it must be fairly small. Otherwise there would be yet a smaller constituent part that we could call the basic cell.

The documents of Puebla[2] explained that the CEB 'is a base-level community because it is composed of relatively few members as a permanent body, like a cell of the larger community'.[3] Some people have criticized this statement for missing the point of why basic communities are called 'basic'. But smallness is one aspect of basicness—far from the whole reason why basic communities are called 'basic', but still one aspect.

[2] See Appendix 1.
[3] Document on *The CEBs, the Parish and the Local Church*, 2.2, (641).

People always ask how big a base community is, and how often it meets. There is no fixed answer, of course, but Leonardo Boff suggests 'fifteen to twenty families' who 'get together once or twice a week to hear the word of God, to share their problems in common, and to solve those problems through the inspiration of the Gospel'.

Dominique Barbé also explains well the fundamentals, explaining why the communities are small, and how small they should be. He is giving an explanation of the three terms *comunidad*, *eclesial* and *de base*.

Groups of human size

As communities, *church base communities are groups of human size, that is, of a size wherein one can learn the name and the history of each member (generally numbering between 20 and 150 persons). In the countryside, the communities average more members than in the city. In the city, the poor, over and above their economic poverty, are uprooted persons, from every corner of the country, who do not know each other. Furthermore, in the city the working schedules are so inhuman that the time available for meeting is much less. In the countryside often, though not always, the misery is greater, but more* time *is available* . . .

The base community is a community and not a group, because all the generations are represented in it: children, young people, adults, old people. There are families; the unmarried; and frequently, visiting guests.

As church-oriented, *the principal motivation of base communities is religious. Practically speaking, all are built around the urban parish in the poor quarters or around the country chapel . . . They represent a church revolution to the extent that they correspond to a gigantic* restructuring *of the Catholic community on the Latin American continent.*

As base communities, *these communities are overwhelmingly made up of people who work with their hands: mothers of families, domestic servants, workers in industry, the unemployed.* . . . .[4]

[4] *Grace and Power — Base Communities and Nonviolence in Brazil*, pp. 88–9.

BASE COMMUNITY IS FOR ALL CULTURES

When did base communities begin? Two kinds of answer can be given. You can say they started somewhere in Brazil sometime in the 1960s (and for more detail on this see p. 121). But this answer is insufficient. It is often said that if you really want to go back to the first basic Christian community you must go back to the community of Jesus and the twelve. Following on from that, the early Church communities were all — properly so-called — basic Christian communities.

Bishop Patrick Kalilombe, back in the early 1970s in Malawi, was writing to his diocese:

> *The Church is called to live and work, in the first and essential place, on this basic community level. From the very beginning of her life (cf. the Acts of the Apostles and the Letters of St Paul) the understanding has been that the Church subsists in such basic communities; the basic local Churches.*[5]

Once it is recognized that basic Christian communities go back to the New Testament, we can see at once that they cannot only be for Latin America (with maybe the Philippines and parts of Africa thrown in as well). They must be for everyone, for all cultures, and all times, and all places. There could not be a form of Church that the third-world Church and the early Church shared in to the exclusion of the other nations.

It may be that the other nations have not yet succeeded in developing authentic base communities yet, at least on any major scale, but that is something different. Our task in the first world is to learn, from those who have gone further along the road than we have, how to rediscover this original vision of what Christian community is all about.

It is often said that base community is a new way of being Church. But if it is also an old way, that goes back to the beginnings, then in a sense there has always been basic ecclesial community, for as long as there has been Church. So, wherever the

[5] *Christ's Church in Lilongwe Today and Tomorrow: Our Diocesan Planning Project,* 28.

⊣ Church is found, basic ecclesial community is found too, in a sense.

And yet in another sense, basic ecclesial community is always in the making, just as the Church is always in the making. Not every part of the Church has really found out what it means to be Church. In fact very few have. And so only a few parts of the Church can strictly be said to have achieved the status of basic ecclesial community.

We should use the term selectively, but not too selectively, or it becomes an impossible ideal. When we want to talk of the ideal (the dream, utopia,[6] etc.) we should talk of the Reign (or the Kingdom).

Basic ecclesial community is a provisional, inadequate structure — but the best we currently have — for working towards the Reign of God, just as Church is a provisional, inadequate structure for working towards the Reign. Church and base community are structures for the journey, not for the final destination. (Even so, at the Seventh Interecclesial Assembly of CEBs in Brazil, one of the speakers did talk of 'the CEB in the sky that awaits us'.)

In this extract from an interview with Daniel Jensen, a Maryknoll priest who began working in Guatemala in 1962, we hear that the first base communities began in New Testament times.

From Jerusalem to Guatemala

If you take the history of basic Christian communities and go back to the first basic Christian communities which were the primitive Christian communities of the New Testament, you find that each one of those communities was different. The basic Christian community of Jerusalem was a community of Jews, who celebrated their prayer life in a Jewish fashion, who followed the Jewish dietary laws, who followed the law of Moses, whereas the basic Christian community that you find later on in Antioch was a group of half pagan, half Jewish people who celebrated its monotheistic faith not in a Jewish manner but in a cultural way that was common to Syria at that time.

[6] For these two terms see Appendix 1.

If you go on to look at the basic Christian community of Corinth, you will find a community of Greeks, who celebrated in a Grecian way their faith in the living Jesus, or if you go to Rome in the first century of the Church, you will find a Roman basic Christian community. Each one of those four places, Jerusalem, Antioch, Corinth, Rome, celebrated their faith in their own way, but no one of them was any better or any worse than the other; they were all basic Christian communities who were celebrating their faith in a manner culturally acceptable to the members of their community.

To that list we could add basic Christian communities of Guatemala. Indian culture is not a western culture, it is a non-western culture. It is not oriental either, but it is a culture all its own. They have their own ways of praying, their own ways of believing, and their own ways of celebrating their faith, of celebrating family, of celebrating being community. For instance, one of the things they do that really creates community is a common sowing of seed. When it comes time to plant, all the men in the community go out together and help one another to plant. Or when it is the time to thatch a roof, all the members of the community get together to help thatch the roof. That's their type of celebration and by their getting together they are creating community. I was giving these as simple examples of what helps to create community.[7]

Some people think that basic Christian communities belong to a different culture from ours — the culture of the third world — so that they would not be appropriate for first-world society; but that is to assume that third-world culture is all of a piece. In fact the communities have been formed successfully in a huge range of cultures. Even within a single country like Brazil there are profound cultural differences from one end of the country to the other, as the next two extracts illustrate. The former is of particular interest because Natal, in Rio Grande do Norte, Brazil, is generally considered to be one of the first places — if not the first place — to develop basic ecclesial communities as they are known today.

[7] The interview, which is with Ian Fraser, is to be found at the Basic Christian Communities Resource Centre at Scottish Churches House, Dunblane, Scotland.

From the south of Brazil to Rio Grande do Norte

*In the beginning the sisters were in a great hurry
and wanted to do a lot in a short time, but as they
thought more about their work they realized that it
is necessary to respect the pace and the different
stages of the people's slow journey and to integrate
oneself totally into that process . . .*

*At the very beginning it was not easy to live this
'inserted'[8] religious life with integrity and balance
because of differences in ways of life, customs and
culture, because the sisters who had come to the
north for this work were from the south of Brazil. It
required a constant effort to give this community life
appropriate expression . . .*

*What made the deepest impression on the people
was the visits the sisters made to their poor houses,
in friendship, and a desire to help them, their
assistance on various occasions, a death, family
problems, and so on. They encouraged people, took
part in their celebrations and talked to everyone,
helping them to discover their values and their
Christian mission. The people were moved by the
charity which had made the sisters leave their
families, possessions and land in the south to come
and live with them.[9]*

This text from a Brazilian booklet for base community meetings
stresses how base communities are a cross-cultural phenomenon.

In each place the CEBs have a different role

*Today we are going to reflect on the role of the
CEBs . . . The CEBs have spread all over Latin
America. We find CEBs in the country and in the
city, in small towns and on the periphery of great*

---

[8] For **insertion** see Appendix 1.
[9] 'Religious Life Among the Poor: The Small Communities of Natal, Rio
Grande do Norte, 1964–1982', *Concilium* 176, p. 57. The sisters come
from the Congregation of the Immaculate Heart of Mary.

*cities, on the coast and in the bush, on hills and in
the lowlands, in sugar-cane plantations and in
metal-work factories. In each place the CEBs have a
different role. . . . in each place, the CEBs confront
different problems and struggles.*

*Besides the differences of place, there also exist
different cultures and different types of work. . . . In
the CEBs we find indians, black people, people of
mixed race, immigrants. There are agricultural
workers, manual workers, laundry workers, casual
workers, domestic workers, fisherfolk. . . . Each has
its own history and its own values. Each has its own
way of being and acting. . . .*

*The path of the local Church also makes the CEBs
different. Some dioceses have been for a long time
on the side of the people, linking the Gospel and
life and struggling for liberation. Others are only
now waking up to this, and some have a lot of
difficulty in understanding this way of being Church.
CEBs themselves progress at different rhythms:*

— *Some are taking their first steps;*
— *others are busy with services and ministries;*
— *others are now acting in pastoral and social work and
in popular movements;*
— *many CEBs now have members engaged in trade
unions and campaigning in political parties.*

*We have seen that the CEBs have very different
roles. But there are also similarities. We are going to
see some points which CEBs have in common:*

— *The active participation of the laity, not only of the
priest;*
— *the growth of new services and ministries;*
— *organization in a form of participatory democracy;*
— *the presence and activity of women;*
— *the struggle for justice and against exploitation;*
— *the Bible in the hands of the people;*
— *the linking of faith and life, present in the
celebrations and in the struggles of the people;*
— *the CEBs, almost always, are formed of ordinary,
poor people.*

. . . In the time of the Apostles it was also like that.

St Paul wrote to the Corinthians (1 Cor 1:26–28):
'Take yourselves, brothers and sisters, at the time
when you were called: how many of you were wise in
the ordinary sense of the word, how many were
influential people, or came from noble families? No,
it was to shame the wise that God chose what is
foolish by human reckoning, and to shame what is
strong that he chose what is weak by human
reckoning; those whom the world thinks common
and contemptible are the ones that God has
chosen—those who are nothing at all to show up
those who are everything.'[10]

BASE COMMUNITY IS FOR EVERYONE IN THE CHURCH

Something that is said over and over again by the liberation theologians is that basic ecclesial communities are 'not a movement'. Often this is expanded to 'they are not a movement within the Church, but rather the Church in movement'.

We might be tempted to think that this is just a way of distancing base communities, which are associated with the left wing, from some of the most powerful movements in the Church today which are associated with the right wing—movements, for example, like Opus Dei or Communion and Liberation. But that is not really the point, for there are also plenty of excellent movements that are not right-wing.

The main point is that base communities are not for particular segments of the Church population, but for everyone. We will return to this point from a different perspective on p. 86 in the chapter on option for the poor, but for the moment the aspect I wish to stress is that in the base community nothing is asked of people by way of membership qualification beyond what the Gospel asks of all Christians.

That is also why they are said to be 'a new way of being Church': they are not an extra organization that keen Church members can join, but they are the basic community, the first and fundamental one. At the end of the 1980s a subtle change began to occur as the phrase 'a new way of being Church' sometimes began to be

---

[10] *Povo de Deus na América Latina a Caminho da Libertação*, 7° Encontro Intereclesial de CEBs, Coleção Fé e Vida, CEBs – 3, pp. 16–19.

rephrased as 'a new way for the Church to be'.[11] The implication became even stronger that the base community way is not just one, optional approach, but a call to the entire Church to live in a different way.

The base communities should impel their members to belong to movements, groups, people's organizations, and other types of interest group. But the base community meeting should be different — it should be more of 'a moment for gathering together the pieces of life', says Carolee Chanona.[12] 'The community does not exist for meetings, but for communion',[13] so that it is not just one more meeting in a busy life of many meetings: it is more like a family meeting around a table at the end of a hard week in the office, in the factory, in the school.

And so base communities are for young and old — and the place of children is always an important factor in them. They are for women and men — although often the women are more numerous and more active. They are for working people and for unemployed, for single people and for couples, for literate and illiterate, for saints and for sinners.

It also follows that they are not an interest group, or a group of friends, or a sort of protest group or ginger group that finds its *raison d'être* as a minority leading the way for the majority. These are all splendid things — interest groups, and groups of friends, and ginger groups. But they are not basic ecclesial communities. They are something different.

Of course the base community will in fact develop interests of its own. The members will in fact become friends. And the community will in fact act as a ginger group for the rest of the Church where base communities are not established. But that again is something different. It may also be that a base community will grow out of a group of friends, or out of a group campaigning for a particular cause. But there is a decisive development there, in the change from interest group to basic cell of the Church. The essence of the basic Christian community is that it is the local Church, acting as it should — as true Church, as true community, as true Christians.

Base communities have come to be associated very much with the locality, but must that necessarily be so? Must the basis for

---

[11] From *um novo modo de ser Igreja* to *um novo modo de Igreja ser*.
[12] A member of José Marins' workshop team.
[13] It sounds better in Spanish: *La comunidad no existe para la reunión, sino la comunión.*

membership be a geographical one, so that the members come from the same small neighbourhood?

Not necessarily: some communities are associated more with the work of the members. Even then there is sometimes a geographical location implied in the place of work: factory workers meet in the factory, fisherfolk meet at the shore. Or there can be a base community that brings together people working at different types of job in the same location, as when the students, janitors, cooks and professors of a college meet in community to share their common Christian faith. Again in Africa it is often the age group that is the natural unit of community; but even so, we would be talking about age groups within a locality.

There are some communities which are based on a particular segment of the population which has special needs that are better met when that group is taken alone. The traditional Church has customarily been prepared to recognize these, through the system of chaplaincies.

For example, the students of a college or university or polytechnic will usually have their own chaplaincy rather than being expected to push their way into a local parish. Frequently immigrant communities are best served by a chaplaincy where their own languages and customs can make them feel at home: there are Caribbean chaplaincies, Chinese chaplaincies, generalized Asian chaplaincies, and so on. Once we have seen how effectively these specialized chaplaincies can work, we can have no hesitations about their validity. Without them the members of these minority groups would be swallowed up in parishes and lose their identity.

In the same way, basic Christian communities can be formed for particular groups with special needs. So we find, for example, Salvadorean base communities in the United States, where the common factor is not the neighbourhood but the country of origin. This makes perfect sense so long as we do not attempt to fit everyone into their own special category. Chaplaincies supplement parishes, and work in relationship with them; they could not supplant them. Neither could base communities for minority groups remove the need for local groups open to all.

The advantage of the geographical basis is that it makes for a community that is more inclusive and less cliquish. What needs to be set against that, however, is the danger of a structure that is too rigid and imposed from the top downwards. The colonial powers made African nations by drawing lines on a map, and they left havoc behind them, for they ended up dividing up tribes that belonged together and jamming together other tribes that were not natural allies. That is not the kind of mapping out that is needed. We may need pastoral planning — sensitively developed and always subject to re-evaluation — but what we do not need is arbitrary authoritarianism.

When geographical communities are formed, they need to respect the naturalness of groupings, so that real communities can develop. There is no reason why there should not be a number of local communities covering the same area, but appealing to people with different needs. It may even be a simple question of elderly people meeting in the day because they do not want to go out at night, while others cannot meet by day because they are at work.

When a community is too homogeneous, then it lacks something of the inclusivity and catholicity of Church and can easily become inturned and intolerant of those with whom it disagrees. But when it is too heterogeneous it will not jell and become community, and is liable to fizzle out very quickly. It is all a question of balance.

In the long run some sort of geographical basis is likely to prove, generally speaking, the most satisfactory foundation for base community membership. If we think of how the Church can divide up its mission throughout the world, so that every person has somewhere to turn, then we are likely to end up by carving up the map — first into dioceses, then into parishes, then into local communities. That way, every place is covered, and through every place, every person is covered too.

Any other basis runs the risk of forgetting someone who does not easily fit into other groups. The Church must forget nobody. And so it is good and right that base communities have come to be associated so very much with the *barrio*, the locality.

This extract from a popular Brazilian booklet stresses the importance of the locality as the basis for Christian community. The community should be open to all the neighbours, rather than being formed of friends and the like-minded. In the first place this text is talking of Reflection Groups, but the text makes clear that the Reflection Group is the first step towards basic ecclesial community.

Some advice about organizing Reflection Groups

1. Neighbouring families

It is of the greatest importance that the people and families invited to form a Reflection Group should

*live near to each other. The families should be
neighbours. This will encourage people to participate
in meetings, as well as fostering a new,
communitarian, brotherly or sisterly way of life. Only
in this way will the Reflection Group be, right from
the beginning, a 'small ecclesial community'.*

2. Members of the Reflection Group

*The members invited to form the Reflection Groups
should be entire families, both parents and children.
And not just married people — still less, just women.
It is true (fortunately) that many Reflection Groups
have begun with just women: later, they have per-
suaded the men and even the children to come. It is
a process which sometimes takes years . . .*

*It is important that families be got to participate
in the Reflection Group in the most natural way
possible. On the one hand, no one should be forced.
But on the other, the door needs to be open to all,
with all human friendship and with all Christian
charity.*

3. Without discrimination

*When neighbouring families are invited to join the
Group, there should be no differentiations made,
least of all in social or economic terms. Christ
destroyed all discrimination and divisions between
people (Galatians 3:26–28). For this reason the colour, race, education, social or economic conditions of
people do not matter and they should not be taken
into consideration . . .*

Reflection Groups sown over the entire parish territory

*With the passing of time, the entire parish area
should be dotted, sprinkled and riddled with
Reflection Groups, so that no one is deprived of the
proclamation of the Gospel.*

*Not one street, block or alley can be forgotten. All
people have the right to hear the Word of God,
since Christ sent the Gospel to be preached to the*

*whole world and to every creature. And if all have
the right to hear it, we have the duty to preach it.*[14]

Contrary to the belief that a base community is by its nature for
'progressive' people, the following passage shows how the most
traditionally-minded churchgoers were perfect material for forming
into basic ecclesial community.

Journey of the CEB of Itápolis

*For generations everything was centred in the parish.
All of a sudden we realized that things could be
different, even in the interpretation of the Gospel.
The people, who began the community, came from
long years of traditional Church, where we were
merely spectators. We would spend a hard week of
struggle, each for himself or herself, in a dry cruel
egoism, and on Sunday we would go to Mass to listen
to the nice readings and take part in those formalized
rituals. Then we would go back home and begin all
over again. We started discovering that a base community had to be different. It had to let people
know one another as people, as children of God.*[15]

BASE COMMUNITY VALUES THE INDIVIDUAL

In societies where there is a strong community ideology it can
sometimes happen that odd individuals feel they do not fit in. Then
there is a conflict between the needs of the individual and the
demands of the community.

Some people would say this happens in communism — where the
common good becomes oppressive of individual freedom. But it
can also happen, for example, in a British public school, where a
failure to behave in the way expected can lead to a charge of letting
down the honour of the school.

---

[14] Dom Joel Ivo Catapan, *Sementes de CEBs: Grupos de Reflexão,
Oração e Ação,* pp. 16–17, 50.
[15] Frances O'Gorman, *Base Communities in Brazil: Dynamics of a
Journey,* pp. 41–2, drawing on *Cadernos da AEC do Brasil,* no. 17 (1983).

A true community, however, is not a mould to which members have to conform. The community finds its identity as a group through recognizing and valuing the identity of each individual member. Properly understood there is no conflict between caring for the individual and caring for the community. In fact, only if there is a genuine community can the individual be cared for and supported.

Some photocopied notes used by Maryknoll missioners, for example, describe the basic ecclesial community as 'A Process of Liberation of Persons . . .', and explains: 'The first vocation of a human being is to be a person; thus CEB greatly stresses the process of personalization. Without this, no great progress in community building is possible. But many persons do not feel free to be who they are.'

A frequent exercise in José Marins' workshop on basic Christian communities is for each individual to spend some time thinking about 'Who am I?' Then they are in a position to tell one other person about themselves, and to listen in turn to 'Who are you?' When several such pairs come together, and each person is introduced with something of their history and something of their dreams, then the group as a whole is able to address the question 'Who are we?' Usually the group is then invited to name itself according to the identity that it has found in common. Though this is a workshop exercise it mirrors a process that must happen if any community is really to be a community.

A community is a space for friendship: it should not pressure us into an intimate divesting, but rather make room for what we want to share among people who respect and welcome us. We cannot argue with another person's story — that is their truth — but we may be challenged to open up to those who are different from us.

The individualism [16] that we sometimes hear denounced by base communities is when the process never moves forward from 'Who am I?' to 'Who are you?', let alone to 'Who are we?' Then you have a lot of selfish people, uninterested in anyone else, jostling for their own position, and not doing anything to help the needs of others.

The point is important, because often we hear criticisms of purely individual spirituality. It would be a mistake to think that because the community dimension is encouraged, therefore private prayer and devotion is discouraged. Both personal and communal spirituality are necessary, and they balance each other. Without the community dimension, spirituality becomes inward-looking and self-centred. Without the personal dimension, the community

---

[16] More is said on **individualism** in Appendix 1.

dimension cannot be born, for a community is made up of persons.

This should reassure those who feel they do not fit well into groups. Usually their discomfort comes because they do not fit in with the prior expectations of the group. A young person who does not like pop music can feel lonely in a youth club. A woman without children can feel isolated in a wives' group where everyone else has a family. A working-class person can feel out of place in a discussion group of highly articulate people.

In a basic ecclesial community there should not be a prior agenda such as to make any individual feel out of place. The Christian community that forms is the community of the Christians who are there, with all their individual personalities intact.

The following extract comes from a book by Dominique Barbé, who has dedicated his life to working with the base communities and the workers of São Paulo. The passage shows how necessary to the formation of community is the first step—that of listening to each person and giving value to each individual.

Nothing interesting today

Among themselves the poor have got into the habit of self-depreciation. What a labourer says has no weight besides the word of an engineer or a priest. 'At least they have studied. You are like us, you know nothing.' How can the world be changed through a people as discouraged as this? That is why each base community is founded through a gentle and gradual pedagogy, which teaches the humble once again to listen to each other and speak to each other in community; to give worth to what they have to say as they express themselves to each other. It is really the miracle of the healing of the deaf-mute once again. Later in this stage we begin to read the Scripture together.

Telling What Happened Today: It is evening at a gathering of the base community, or a study day. Each one describes his or her day from morning till evening. Very often at the beginning we hear something like this: 'Who, me? Nothing interesting. As usual. Washing the laundry. Cooking . . .' She has let the word slip out: nothing interesting. It is

22

> *important for a mother of a family to be able to tell*
> *what time she got up; how many times she got up*
> *during the night or at dawn to give the bottle to the*
> *baby, to heat the coffee for her husband who is*
> *going off to the factory, to fix the lunch-box for her*
> *oldest son who leaves later, to get the children ready*
> *for school. We go around the table and each one is*
> *able to describe the day that has just finished.*[17]

BASE COMMUNITY IS A PROCESS, WITH UPS AND DOWNS

Curiously, one of the most comforting things for a first-world person to hear about base communities is about their failures. Given the considerable difficulties in bringing about this new way of being Church in the developed nations, it is good to know that the third world has met many of the same problems. Otherwise one can get the impression that it would all be so much easier if one lived on the other side of the equator, but over here it really is impossible.

There is always the temptation to think of a base community as something instant, which will just pop up by itself in the right combination of circumstances. The truth is that basic Christian community is not so much a state as a process. It takes time to reach the moment of awareness of which Carolee Chanona speaks: 'a community truly becomes a basic Christian community when it becomes aware that it is a basic cell of the Church'. And even the well-established communities are still in process, as they live through their ups and downs. No community is brought to birth without a lot of hard work.

Hearing the things that go wrong can bring one back to earth, and give one the commitment and staying power to launch on what is—anywhere in the world—a long and time-consuming process.

Here is an animator from a base community in Mexico City, recounting his story:

[17] *Grace and Power*, p. 97.

Only the coordinators were left

*I joined a Basic Ecclesial Community just as anybody
else would and I have now been six years in these
communities. These particular communities were
started off by some seminarians; then they went off
and after that they came back only once a week.
After seven weeks, I ended up as animator of my
community. When all this began, there were four
communities but after the seminarians left and the
priest lost interest, the communities began to
disintegrate and, eventually, there were only the
coordinators left and so we decided to form one
community amongst ourselves. After three years we
again began to establish other communities and by
now we knew for certain that the priest was not with
us. Today, just as at the very beginning, there are
four communities and I am in charge of one of
them.*[18]

Uriel Molina is well known for his work among some of the most
lively, active and radical of Nicaragua's youth, and today his church
is a favourite spot for visitors to go and hear the vigorous *Misa
Campesina*. But in this passage we hear how unpromising the
outlook seemed at first, in 1965. An inability to get going on scripture reflection is also one of the problems most often found among
ordinary Catholics in the first world.

The problems of Bible-study

*The Franciscans had built the church, the religious
house and a dispensary. Their pastoral activity had
been in the traditional mould. I decided, therefore,
to start work along the lines suggested by the Second
Vatican Council, which had just come to an end. I
began to invite the faithful to meet me, so that I
could explain to them what was needed in these
modern days, and these meetings gradually
developed into a regular Bible School, which went
on for about ten years.*

[18] Carlos Zarco Mera, Concilium 176, p. 65.

My first sessions of the Bible were limited to providing introductory material and replying to criticisms. A little later we worked through a course on the History of Salvation. The task was not an easy one. Those simple people, weary from their day's work, illiterate, and accustomed only to a folk-lore type of Catholicism, were not able properly to tackle Bible-study. But they were very willing, and with the help of biblical maps and colour-slides they learnt about the land where Jesus lived, and so acquired a real desire to get to know the Bible.[19]

The next extract comes from a recorded conversation I had with Jorge Marskell, Bishop of the Itacoatiara diocese in the Manaus region of Brazil:

Like the phases of the moon

MH: How developed are the basic ecclesial communities in your diocese?

JM: In some areas they have had a history of a caminhada — of a journey — over a number of years. In newer areas of the prelacy, where they are just beginning — a little weaker. I like what Clodovis Boff[20] says about basic Christian communities: they are like the phases of the moon. I can visit basic Christian communities along a river, say one month, and maybe six months from now I go back and make another visit. When I'm there this time, I'll find a lot of them very full of life and energy and really willing to go. And others are desanimado, down in the dumps — 'What do we do? Where do we go from here?' When I go back six months from now, those that were really on a high will be in the dumps, and those that were low, because of the visit the previous six months ago, will be really animated. So they are like the phases of the moon.

---

[19] Concilium 176, p. 3.
[20] Brother of Leonardo Boff.

Leonardo Boff here records the stages of development in a basic ecclesial community. Many others have noticed the same process of growth—from just a scripture reflection group, to a true basic ecclesial community, participating first religiously, then socially, then politically.

The stages of a CEB

The people themselves took responsibility for their destiny. This generally began with reading the Bible and proceeded to the creation of small base or basic ecclesial communities. Initially, such a community serves to deepen the faith of its members, to prepare the liturgy, the sacraments, and the life of prayer. At a more advanced stage these members begin to help each other. As they become better organized and reflect more deeply, they come to the realization that the problems they encounter have a structural character.[21]

Dominique Barbé gives some idea of the length of time that should be allowed for this process.

Ten years to maturity

A base community evolves very slowly. In our opinion, it takes ten years for it to arrive at maturity. Does it not take about the same time to train a priest, a doctor, an engineer? Priests have at least six years of seminary, not counting periods of review and supplementary studies. It is at least as difficult to shape a Christian community as to train its members—at least if we really want it to hold together.[22]

[21] *Church, Charism and Power*, p. 8.
[22] *Grace and Power*, p. 105.

THE CHURCH IS NOT THE BUILDING OR THE CLERGY BUT THE PEOPLE

Few of us would admit to thinking that the Church meant the building or the clergy, yet old habits die hard. We are still more influenced by this way of thinking than we like to admit.

Our language is constantly giving us away. We 'go to church', meaning going to the building, not meeting with the other parishioners in some other venue. And someone 'goes into the church' when he or she decides to become ordained.

There is little point in protesting that we have really left behind such old ways of thinking: we know well from the insights of the feminist movement, among many others, that the way we talk influences, and is influenced by, the way we think.

More useful is to let our ear become attuned to when those building-centred or clergy-centred habits of speech are still operating, so at least we can notice how our minds are working.

There is a true story about a first-world parish that illustrates what I mean.

What is a parish mass?

A new priest moved to a rather dead parish. He was energetic and keen. Up the road from the parish church was a convent. For some years now, the convent had opened its doors at 11.00 on a Sunday morning to anyone who would like to attend their mass. Down the road the parish church also had a mass at 11.00 a.m.

The new priest visited the sisters soon after he arrived. They had tea together, each side gently trying to size up the other. The sisters wanted a better, more collaborative relationship with the new priest than they had had before. The new priest wanted to build up his parish.

'How do you see the role of sisters in a parish?' asked the nuns tentatively. 'I see them at the very heart of parish life', said the priest confidently. Both sides breathed a sigh of relief.

By the end of tea-time the sisters had offered,

without prompting, to discontinue their 'rival show'.
A happy ending? Or are there more questions to be
answered?

Such as: what about the people? Those who had
chosen to attend a mass in a different place, said by
a different priest, presumably had reasons for their
choice. It may have been that they liked the cosy
ambience of the little chapel, rather than the bleak
emptiness of the parish church. It may have been
that they found greater opportunities to contribute
to the liturgy there. It might have been that they
appreciated the chance to mingle with the sisters and
were encouraged by their example and commitment;
or that they had formed supportive relationships with
the other priest, or with their fellow mass-goers.

There is another line the new parish priest could
have taken. If the parish is the people — not the
building, not the priest — then he could have
recognized the mass in the convent, said by another
priest, as an authentic part of parish life. Instead of
treating it as a rival show — because it was not in his
building, said by him — he could have welcomed and
advertised the alternative mass as a part of the lively
variety of parish activities.

He could not, perhaps, have moved the other
parishioners down to join the convent at 11.00: the
chapel was too small for that. But he could have
shown that he had a broader view of where the
parish was than the parish church, and a broader
view of who the parish was than the parish priest.

There is a story from somewhere in Latin America, that makes us
realize how easily we identify Church with clergy. A group of
peasants from a base community were going to the municipal
authorities, accompanied by their priest, in pursuit of rights which
were being denied them. When they had finished putting their
case, the mayor turned to the priest. 'And what does the Church
think?' he asked. 'You have just heard what the Church thinks',
he replied.

As for identifying Church with a building, the next story comes
from Chile. Leonardo Boff observed that Church is an event that
may happen underneath a mango tree. We may be inspired also

by the example of a base community that met for six years in a disused bus — quite a satisfactory venue for twenty people. Others meet in houses, garages, multi-purpose halls, . . . and of course church buildings.

St Peter's Parish

In Santiago, Chile, someone arrived from abroad to visit a priest-friend who lived in St Peter's Parish on the outskirts of the city. He took a bus out to the area. He didn't have the exact address — all he knew was that the priest lived in the parish. However, the parish church ought to have a steeple, so it was simply a case of looking for the steeple above the roof-tops.

Dusk was coming on. As it got darker it was becoming difficult to locate the steeple. He needed to find someone who could point him in the right direction. There was a small bar open. He went in.

'Could you please tell me where St Peter's Church is?' he asked.

'The Church of St Peter meets today in the home of the Lopez family', a man in the bar answered.[23]

THE BASE COMMUNITY IS IN COMMUNION WITH THE UNIVERSAL CHURCH

There is no misunderstanding more widespread than that base communities are an alternative, parallel, breakaway, underground, go-it-alone, anti-institutional kind of Church community. Because of the large degree of space that the base communities have made for themselves — their initiatives in mission and ministry, their freedom in interpreting scripture, their sense of being Church — it is often assumed that they are self-sufficient and independent of any outside authority.

On the contrary, they see themselves as very much part of the one, united Church, in communion with their clergy, their bishops and the Pope. The liberation theologians make quite clear the need

---

[23] José Marins, Teolide Maria Trevisan, Carolee Chanona, *The Church from the Roots: Basic Ecclesial Communities*, p. 8.

to remain in that communion. Even as fierce a critic of Roman authoritarianism as Leonardo Boff has made his allegiance and fidelity abundantly clear. When he received notification that the Congregation for the Doctrine of the Faith was planning moves to discipline him, he said 'I prefer to walk with the Church rather than to walk alone with my theology'.[24]

Of course there is no denying that there has been massive conflict between the communities and the hierarchy. Parish priests have caused problems for local communities, and bishops have caused problems for priests who are promoting base communities. Where the priests and bishops are not favourable it becomes very difficult for the communities to operate, and there has been a lot of ill feeling and disappointment. Partly the difficulties are a matter of misunderstanding and caution, but there is also a fundamental clash between a view of Church that is carefully supervised from the top down and a view of Church in which the people are encouraged to take on responsibility for themselves. It can happen that the hierarchy says all the right things on paper and yet almost totally suppresses the spirit of the communities in practice, because they have not yet internalized a non-clericalist way of operating.

Yet none of this would matter to the base communities if they felt themselves to be independent groups anyway. The tension and the hurt arises precisely because they cannot conceive of breaking away. The members of base communities are simple, ordinary people who love their priest, who love their bishop, who love their Pope. As Teolide Trevisan[25] has pointed out, it is the support of the priest which gives to the ordinary people of the base community the assurance that they are really Church. And so it is this link with the institution that gives the community the space and support in which to grow and discover how much they can do by themselves.

The more poor, humble and uneducated the people are, the less likely they are to start an initiative in protest against their local pastors. But given the encouragement of their Church leaders, it is wonderful to find how much the people are capable of.

[24] See Harvey Cox, *The Silencing of Leonardo Boff*, p. 105. Even though Leonardo Boff resigned from the priesthood and the Order of Friars Minor in June 1992, he remains of course a Catholic layman. He found a different way in which he could continue to 'walk with the Church', rather than to step outside it. His statement said: 'I am leaving the priestly ministry and the Franciscan Order not to be free from the Church, which I love and shall never abandon, but to be free to work without impediment.'

[25] A member of José Marins' travelling workshop team.

Not surprisingly, then, we find that where, in fact, the bishops have encouraged them, base communities have developed well and fast. And where the bishops have discouraged the growth of base communities, they have not got far at all. Where there is not even encouragement from clergy or religious, they have rarely even begun.

This passage from Leonardo Boff's *Ecclesiogenesis* reports back on the Fourth Interecclesial Assembly of CEBs in Itaici, Brazil in 1981.

No breach with the institution

Unlike what many might have thought, there was nothing about the participants to indicate any threat of breach with the oneness of the church. On the contrary, with great maturity and critical distance, the participants discussed tensions existing among various pastoral approaches, the resistance of some to accepting the approach of a people who become People of God by way of the basic communities, or the authoritarian attitudes of certain bishops who still cling to a triumphalist conceptualization of church. Such obstacles were viewed as inevitable on any journey, hence not to be taken too dramatically. The plenary assembly voted to write the pope a letter, thanking him for the greeting he had addressed to the communities in Manaus, and containing a declaration of loyalty to the great apostolic tradition whose guarantor the pope was.[26]

Another passage from *Ecclesiogenesis* gives a more theological background to the reasons why schisms and splinter-groups are not on the agenda.

Visible communion

Communion can be expressed in many symbols or few. It can take different forms of visibility. But it must be present in the churches. Without it they

[26] *Ecclesiogenesis*, p. 37.

would not be churches. Therefore communion is an indivisible reality, not admitting of degree. Communion either is present or is not present. *Communion among all the churches is expressed by symbols that translate and reinforce this union. The heads of local churches, besides constituting a principle of internal unity, constitute as well a principle of oneness with the other churches: the head of the basic community, the pastor of the parish, the bishop of the diocese, the pope of the whole church. A single creed, the same basic structures of liturgy, of juridical ordination, of theological understanding form instances of the expression of the unity, the oneness, of all the churches.*[27]

Another witness from Brazil, Frances O'Gorman, speaking at a summer school on base communities, stressed the same point to a largely first-world audience. (The passage is transcribed from a video recording of the event.)

Raising questions from inside

Base communities do not necessarily mean rupture with the established Church. On the contrary, it is essential to be within the established Church . . . to have that confidence in belonging to a universal Church and to a Church in communion with other Churches.

The base communities are the charism within the institutional Church. They help the Church not be monolithic. They give it the healthy youthfulness of the Church. They keep it open, young, in movement . . . As committed Christians in the base communities within the Church, they try to bring about the conversion of the Church structures . . . So they are a force of the Church moving, not a movement within.

One of the examples of the total conversion of a Church structure is the yearly assembly, the assembly of the People of God as they call it. You have in a diocese, for example, representatives from each of the traditional groups in the Church and a

---

[27] Ecclesiogenesis, p. 22.

*representative from each one of the base communities.
Since there are so many base communities, you
would then have a great representation from the
people. But there still is a voice for the traditional
groups within the parish or the diocese.*

*What do they do? They evaluate the past year of
the pastoral plan*[28] *and make suggestions for the
coming year. They raise criticisms, they raise
suggestions. The bishops listen and take that into
account and make their plans with all of these
inputs . . .*

*The idea of this conversion is that the fruit of the
base communities influences the diocesan structure.
So we stay inside to raise questioning, not move out
and question from the outside.*[29]

THE BASE COMMUNITY IS A EUCHARISTIC
COMMUNITY

If basic ecclesial community is not just a group of Christians
meeting together, but actually a basic cell of the Church, then all
the basic elements for being Church must be found at the grassroots
level. Of course the Church can take all sorts of different forms in
different times and places, and all these different aspects cannot
possibly be represented within one base community. But what must
be found there is some recognizable presence of the essentials —
those characteristics without which a church would not be a church.

One of the essential characteristics of Church is the eucharist. If
the basic ecclesial community is the basic cell of the Church, then
surely it must have the eucharist? After all, do not even the most
respectable Church documents tell us that the Church is centred
around the eucharist? Vatican II tells us that 'No Christian community can be built up unless it has its basis and centre in the
celebration of the most Holy Eucharist'.[30]

Yet, as is well known, very many basic ecclesial communities do
not have a priest available to say mass on a regular basis, and only

---

[28] See **pastoral planning** in Appendix 1.
[29] Summer school organized by the Oxford Centre for Mission Studies,
August 1985.
[30] Presbyterorum Ordinis, 6.

a priest is allowed to preside at a eucharist. So the pressure builds up for that rule to be relaxed, so that every basic ecclesial community can indeed have its basis and centre in the celebration of the eucharist.

This is one of the most thorny issues, and people easily become agitated in their allegiance to one point of view or another. It is a key point, where differing views of base communities come to a head, and where some first-world communities branch off from the practice and theology that is prevalent in the third world.

A Latin American base community would typically cope with the situation by exploring the maximum that can be done within current Church discipline. Frequently the solution is to have a communion service led by a lay eucharistic minister, using pre-consecrated hosts. Sometimes a symbolic meal would be shared that would be seen as an *agape* — that is, a love-feast, or symbolic sharing of food and drink, that does not claim to be eucharistic. And often, again, the solution would be to explore other forms of worship — liturgies that would come under the general heading of 'Celebrations of the Word', in which you have the freedom to do practically anything you like except celebrate the eucharist. Then, when the priest was able to visit, they would make a really big celebration of that mass.

And so the third-world approach would be in conformity with the aspirations of the great meeting of Latin American bishops at Medellín,[31] that the basic ecclesial communities should 'in so far as possible, find their fulfilment in the Eucharistic celebration, always in communion with and dependent upon the local bishop'.[32] In short, they should and do have the eucharist; but that does not mean they have to be celebrating it every time they meet.

At the same time the third-world base communities might press for a change of the Church's discipline concerning ordination, asking for the ordination of base-community coordinators who were not eligible under the present rules — either because they were married, or because they were women, or because they were not able to spend years of full-time study in a seminary. But pressing for change is quite different from going ahead with celebrating the eucharist without authorization.

Some first-world groups, on the other hand, would go further. Some (but of course not all) first-world communities would see the

---

[31] For **Medellín** see Appendix 1.
[32] *Pastoral Care of the Masses*, 13.

Church rules as wrong, not only because they deprive so many Christians of the frequent reception of the sacrament, but also on principle because they believe that the power to celebrate the eucharist comes from within the community and not from outside. And so, for example, the US writer Virginia Hoffman speaks of eucharist without clergy as 'Cutting the Cord: Restoring Eucharist to the Community'.[33] And a member of La Traboule community, Lyons, France, is recorded as saying 'When the priest cannot be there to celebrate the eucharist, the community celebrates the eucharist itself, because it is quite clear that the eucharist is an act of the whole community'.[34]

In reply it should be pointed out that in Catholic theology the eucharist is always (at least in theory) celebrated by the whole community: the priest presides, but the whole people celebrate together. But a recognized, ordained person is needed to preside, to enable the eucharist to be an act of the universal Church, and not just an act of the small community physically present.

If the eucharist is to be 'one bread, one body' with the rest of the Church, it is necessary that the Church as a whole recognizes the validity of the act. A small group cannot unilaterally declare that their act is an act of the whole Church, if the rest of the Church does not accept it as such.

There are actually very few acts that are limited to the priest within Catholic theology. Saying the words of consecration is one them. (The words of consecration are 'This is my body . . . This is the cup of my blood . . .') Giving sacramental absolution is another, which is needed to reconcile someone in a state of mortal sin[35] to the Christian community. (The words of sacramental absolution are 'I absolve you from all your sins . . . .')

These two acts are solemn acts of the whole Church, and as such require an official representative who is recognized outside of the local community as well as inside it. The priest who is sometimes described as being 'parachuted in' for the eucharist, is the pledge of communion with the universal Church. It is this that gives sense to celebrating the sacrament of the universal Church. 'Setting up a rival altar' has long been regarded as one of the classic definitions of going into schism.

This is the explanation of what seems to some an inconsistency.

---

[33] *Birthing a Living Church*. This is the title of her ch. 9.
[34] Quoted in two of Ian Fraser's books, *Living a Countersign*, p. 40, and in *Wind and Fire*, p. 92.
[35] For **mortal sin** see Appendix 1.

On the one hand the base communities believe God is to be found at the heart of the community and not just mediated downwards through the hierarchy. On the other hand, they do not take advantage of that presence of God among them to go ahead with celebrating the eucharist alone. Discovering that God is found at the heart of their own community, does not mean that God is *only* to be found there, and that God is not *also* made present to them through other people, through other communities, and through the network of the universal Church.

Apart from consecrating and absolving, there is practically nothing else that cannot validly be done by a layperson — sometimes with special permission, but often without the need for that. The basic ecclesial communities are beginning to make as much practical use as possible of the latitude that the Catholic rules permit. Laity can instruct and teach, even preach; they can baptize; they can lead prayers; they can coordinate groups; they can construct liturgies; they can distribute communion; they can even (in certain circumstances) preside at weddings and funerals.

Enlarging the categories of people who can be ordained is definitely an issue that needs to be worked on. Speaking of the rules for eucharist and ordination, José Marins says 'We are trying to change it, but to change it in a communion.' In the meantime, 'we make the option of keeping communion with Rome.'[36]

A more immediate issue is to implement all the possibilities for lay ministry that are available in the Church, and that are not made use of. This is the agenda on which the base communities have concentrated their efforts.

This passage by Dominique Barbé reaffirms many of the theological points I have made about a Catholic understanding of the eucharist.

[36] Speaking at one of his workshops in Birmingham, in 1987. From time to time people produce examples of Catholic base communities in Latin America that are thought to be celebrating the eucharist without a priest. Often, on examination, there turns out to be a misunderstanding about what they are doing, and it is found they are celebrating a liturgy of the Word, or just distributing communion (which lay people are allowed to do), or having some kind of an agapeic breaking of bread. Very occasionally there are reports of an agape so close to the celebration of the Last Supper, that there does seem some ambiguity over the status of the celebration. (L. Boff discusses some of the finely-tuned distinctions regarding sacramental conditions on p. 73 of *Ecclesiogenesis*, together with a plea for a change in the rules.)

This whole question re-surfaces in the context of discussing the place of the hierarchy; see pp. 135–40 below.

The eucharistic ministry

*At this writing [1982] there are 80,000 base
communities in Brazil. How can it be expected that
the priests on active duty could be available to them
on a regular basis when there are only 12,000 priests
to serve the whole country? It would therefore be
only logical, in view of the dynamic that led to the
creation of so many base communities in the first
place, that they should be granted the right and
option of choosing from among themselves the one
to preside over the Eucharist, the minister, the 'elder'
in experience of life, who would have the duty of
manifesting through ministry the eucharistic maturity
of the community, that is, its ecclesial fullness . . .*

*If it really is an authentic assembly of the
followers of Jesus, it is evident that it has within it
the natural aptitude to celebrate the Holy Supper.
Certainly that will not and cannot happen except in
agreement with the universal Church. We shall
return to this point in an instant . . .*

*The ministry of the one who watches over unity in
the fellowship, in all the senses of the word (unity
with respect to God, the neighbour, other
communities, and the tradition of the apostles), is so
essential that* that person alone *in the Church can
preside over the Eucharist, the sacrament of unity.*

*One deviation would be to underestimate the role
of the ordained minister. In fact there seems no
evidence, however far we go back into the history of
primitive Christianity, that the Mass was ever celebrated
without the presence of an ordained minister . . .*

The bishop, as the name (epi-skopos) *implies, is
the one who 'watches over' unity; this task is so
important that in the beginning the Eucharist seems
normally only to have been celebrated when presided
over by the bishop in person. Today the priest
represents the bishop in the liturgy, since in fact the
priest exercises a ministry of episcopal type and there
is only a difference of degree, not of nature, between
priest and bishop. Nevertheless* one single *bishop
presides at the communion in a diocese.*

*Another deviation also must be avoided: we
cannot say that it is ordained ministers who con-
secrate the bread and wine by themselves. All the
baptized, by virtue of their own baptism, participate
actively in the Holy Supper; all say the* epiclesis *by
which the Holy Spirit is invoked as sanctifier to come
on the assembly and on the symbols that are to
become the body and blood of Christ. Both parties
are concelebrants or, according to a Trappist monk of
the twelfth century,* co-consecrators. *(The writer is
indebted here and throughout this chapter to Hervé
Legrand, OP.).* [37]

This chapter ends with accounts of three different types of liturgy,
to illustrate something of the range of possibilities.

When I was visiting Brazil, I attended a communion service with
pre-consecrated hosts, on the northern outskirts of São Paulo. This
is what happened.

Sunday morning communion service

*We met in a little chapel on a hillside. From the
door you could look for miles over the great expanse
of São Paulo stretching away through the hazy air.
The chapel was very simple: there were some plastic
chairs arranged in a few rows, and two bare light
bulbs hanging from the ceiling. There was a table at
the front, covered in an altar-cloth, with a candle
and a small statue on it. There was a board with
photos stuck on it, and a crucifix on the back wall.*

*A few people had met on the Saturday to prepare
for the liturgy. A group of four catechists took it in
turns to lead it. On the day I was there it was a
young man called Francisco, very simple and eager.
There was a sister present who acted as animator in
the community, but she never led the liturgy: that
was always done by local people. The congregation
was well mixed in terms of age, with several couples
and young children.*

Francisco used a printed mass sheet, which he

---

[37] Grace and Power, pp. 109–12.

*more or less followed, but he missed out the section
that included the consecration. Everyone participated
in the bidding prayers, as people suggested people or
causes to pray for. And everyone participated in the
sermon, which the catechist led in dialogue mode.
The gospel for the day was the Good Samaritan, and
the message Francisco focused on was a very simple
one that went straight to the point. What is God?
God is love, right? And we should love our
neighbour as God loves us, and as the parable tells
us to love, should we not? People joined in with
reflections about what it was like when you passed
people in the street, they greeted you or did not
greet you, and so on.*

*When it came to communion, the hosts were
taken out of a little plastic box such as might have
contained sandwiches. I had perhaps expected more
formality, but I remembered that in many parts of
Brazil the climate makes it difficult to prevent hosts
going mouldy. Perhaps in the circumstances this was
the most appropriate way of keeping them.*

*After the liturgy various groups gathered for
meetings, including a big group of young people
sitting in a circle in the yard outside. They were
having a catechetical session of preparation for
confirmation. I sat on a wall and talked to one of
the young girls of the community. I asked her what
were the main problems in the* barrio. *'Housing', she
said, 'then abandoned children, health, transport
. . . Oh, there is no lack of problems. Life here is
difficult. But I think life is difficult everywhere.'*

Without a priest, another possibility is a Celebration of the Word.
This Celebration which I attended, in San Salvador, shows how free
you can be when you get away from assuming that every liturgy
should be eucharistic.

A real celebration

*I took a bus with a number of young people from
the local base communities, who had been invited to
join with youth from other communities for a*

'Celebration of the Word'. The venue was a dusty clearing in a wood, where the most primitive seating had been constructed—mostly logs to sit on, arranged in a circle. There were some balloons hung up between the trees, to make it festive. All through the celebration, dogs, chickens and cows wandered freely around us in the wood.

The event was supposed to begin at 2.00. In fact it got going at 3.30, first with a song, accompanied by a guitar, and then with a welcome and some getting-to-know-each-other exercises. In the first of these we were each given a yellow strip of paper with half a proverb on it: someone else had the missing half, and you had to hunt around till you found them. Then we sat down again in new places.

Now we were told to make sure we knew the name of the person on either side of us. Someone stood in the middle and pointed around the circle in an arbitrary fashion: if they cried 'pineapple!' you had to give the name of the person on your right; if it was 'orange!' you had to give the name on the left; and if it was 'all change!' you had to leap up and rush to a new seat. All very uproarious, but this was not a prelude to the celebration—it was the first part of it.

When everyone was loosened up and knew everyone else, one of the organizing group gave a short address. Then we stood in the circle and held hands for a spontaneous prayer of thanksgiving. Next came the penitential part of the liturgy. We were all given a scrap of paper and invited to write a sin on it, and then to put it in a tin where a little fire had been lit. We said goodbye to our sins like this. Then we were invited to share with our neighbours some reflections on what we had done. This might have been quite an undertaking in a group of people you had never met before, if we had not had such a long, giggly warm-up at the start.

Now once again a few people were asked to change places—to break up one or two little groups of bosom friends who had come together and were resisting mixing in with the rest of the group. Then we had the first reading, which was from Jeremiah.

*After it was read, it was read again, to make sure we
had taken it in. Then we got into groups of five, to
discuss it. After ten minutes' chat, we shared our
thoughts in plenary.*

*Now we stood up again and had a lively song, and
after that came the Gospel. This time we reflected on
it straightaway as a big group. Then came another
couple of songs, and the sharing of the peace, and
we went round the clearing hugging each other.*

*Now came refreshments — which I suppose made it
a sort of agape, though there was no ritual attached.
We had fragments of broken biscuits — they were not
broken to symbolize breaking, they were just broken
scraps anyway, for these were very poor people. And
there was a cold drink, one of the typical drinks of
the poor in El Salvador, a diluted drink with a sort
of cereal content, whitish in colour.*

*After that and a lot of chat, we joined hands in a
circle again for a prayer of thanks, and then sang the
Our Father. Finally there was a photo. The logs were
piled up and people scrambled up to make a group
picture. It was very hilarious, because every time we
thought we had got everyone in, one of the logs at
the back collapsed and people went shooting off
them. But at last the snap was taken. The whole
Celebration had taken nearly three hours — in
addition, of course, to the late start.*

*What impressed me most was the way the young
people could move from the laughter and fun of the
beginning, to very serious reflection and prayer:
there was much said in the context of the difficult
and dangerous times in the country, and of the need
for courage and commitment to the way of Christ.*

Lastly we have an account of an actual eucharist.

Carolee Chanona[38] likes to stress that though the eucharist is
important to a base community, what is more important is discovering what it means to be a eucharistic community. So it is not a question of having the eucharist as often as possible, but making sure

---

[38] See p. 16 above.

that when there is a eucharist, it really means what the eucharist should mean. Frequency is not so important, but quality is.

I could tell about the mass I went to in a tiny hut on a hillside in Matagalpa, Nicaragua, among the Mothers of Heroes and Martyrs—one of the most beautiful masses I have ever attended. But instead I have chosen this account by James Pitt of a mass in São João de Meriti, Rio de Janeiro, because of the impression it made on him about the meaning of the eucharist.

Mass for a wedding anniversary

This community consists of about 20 families (somewhere between 120–160 people). They have their chapel which is more of a community centre and meeting place than a church where they meet each Sunday morning to celebrate the Word—that is read the Gospel, reflect on it, sing hymns and pray.

The day I was there one of the couples was celebrating 25 years of marriage. On a special occasion like this they have a eucharist. The whole celebration was joyful, informal and very spiritual. Lasting about two hours, it included a good hour's discussion about marriage. People shared experiences both good and bad, and began to analyze the causes of marriage problems—people forced to work long hours for low pay, the struggle for decent housing, the impossible costs of doctors and medicines.

The priest, who had not given any sort of sermon, very gently deepened the discussion. Why is it necessary to work long hours for low pay? The discussion could have gone on for three hours, but there will be other opportunities. (I asked the priest about sermons. 'Me?' he said, 'Tell them? About marriage? You must be joking! I haven't preached a sermon since I left the seminary.')

I cannot describe the joy, seriousness and spirituality of that eucharist. It gave real meaning to the words 'For where two or three meet in my name, I shall be there with them.' I learned more about the eucharist than from any book, discussion or mass I had previously attended.

Members of this basic community are a dynamic

*force in the neighbourhood. They really are the
leaven — through discussing neighbourhood problems
and the Gospel together, people experience a clear
call to action. I was privileged to share in their
celebration of Christ's presence in their midst.*[39]

[39] James Pitt, *Good News to All*, p. 12.

2

Base community is about the basics of Christianity

In the first chapter we looked at aspects of what it meant to say 'base community is the basic cell of the Church' — what I have called the first mark of basic ecclesial community. This second chapter will explore different aspects of the second mark — 'base community is about the basics of Christianity'.

BASE COMMUNITY IS ABOUT BRINGING TOGETHER FAITH AND LIFE

The base communities bring together faith and life. That lies at the heart of what Christianity is all about. It is the simplest way of putting what is sometimes expressed in more detail as the pastoral cycle, with its sequence of experience, social analysis, theological reflection and action.

The Argentine Bishop Enrique Angelelli[1] used to say that we have two ears and one mouth. With one ear we listen to the people, with the other ear we listen to the Word of God, and then with our mouth we can speak the prophetic message.

[1] Bishop of La Rioja, martyred on 4 August 1976 in a 'car accident'.

Some people think that Church is all about *going to church* and saying prayers together. But that is a travesty of Church, a one-sided conception that is hideously distorting. There must also be commitment, faith into action.

Conversely, some people think that base communities are all about social action. But if the social action is divorced from faith and worship, then you no more have a basic ecclesial community than if you had a group that does nothing more than go to church. There must be some kind of praying together and faith-sharing.

José Marins tells the story of one base community, that seemed at first to be going so well. It was situated in a new *barrio* that was very poor. The people met together, talked, planned and acted. Their great campaign was to get electricity for the *barrio*. They were a very active, committed, lively group. One day they succeeded in their campaign. Electricity was brought to the *barrio*. And what happened to the basic Christian community? Everyone stayed at home and watched television.

What we learn from this story is that action is not enough to make a basic ecclesial community. Christian faith is not just a stepping stone to getting electricity, a lever towards social change. There must be more to a basic Christian community than social action, something more lasting and fundamental.

On the outskirts of São Paulo I met two US Sisters of the Resurrection, Jackie and Laura, who were struggling with the same problem. The basic ecclesial community in their *favela* had been lively and active as long as the road was not asphalted, as long as there was no water and no electricity and no buses. Now they had achieved all those things, the people were much lazier about coming to community meetings.

But, Jackie and Laura said, it is making us examine much more deeply what basic ecclesial community is all about. It is throwing us back on discovering people's ongoing religious needs which never go away. It is a stage for deepening and strengthening the community, rather than a set-back.

One good thing, they said, is that through their experiences with the needs of the *favela*, the people have come to realize that nothing will get done unless they do it, and that is beginning to be expressed in a greater readiness to take responsibility in the Church.

People may come together initially to a community for all sorts of reasons, which are not necessarily particularly religious. They may come because they are lonely, or because they need a school for their children, or because they like singing. There is no right reason for coming in the first place. But if the community is to mature, the reasons for coming must deepen, as the people explore what it means to be basic Christian community.

This first quotation expresses the need for faith and life to come together before genuine Church is born. The speaker is the Maryknoll priest Daniel Jensen whom we met on p. 11 above.

Faith, service and worship

Three of the marks of the basic Christian community are that it be a community of faith, of service and of worship, and I find that if, in any community, you do not have those three elements of faith, service to one another and worship, then it really is not a basic ecclesial community, is not really a Christian community — it is lop-sided, it has lost some of the elements that Jesus came to preach, and it even loses some of its humanness if it loses one of those three elements.[2]

Next we have a passage from Leonardo Boff that reminds us that the political activity of a base community should not take over from its essentially religious character:

Not a political entity

The base ecclesial community does not become a political entity. It remains what it is: a place for the reflection and celebration of faith. But, at the same time, it is the place where human situations are judged ethically in the light of God. The Christian community and the political community are two open spheres where what is properly Christian circulates. The community celebrates and is nourished by its faith; it hears the word of God that engenders a commitment to one's brothers and sisters. In the political community one works and acts side by side

---

[2] This interview with Ian Fraser can be found in the Basic Christian Communities Resource Centre at Scottish Churches House, Dunblane.

*with others, concretely realizing faith and salvation,
listening to God's voice which is fully expressed in
the Christian community.*[3]

If Boff reminds us that action without faith is not enough, Dominique Barbé tells this story to remind us that faith without action is
not enough either.

Building the widow's house

*Now we arrive at the decisive moment in the birth
of a church base community. Everything we have
said until now is preliminary. A group does not
become a community until the day it decides to act
together, to pass to action. Mission creates unity.
Action permits a verification of whether or not the
word has truly taken on flesh. We must leave Egypt
in order to journey toward the Promised Land; the
exodus of action is always necessary.*

*As for us, our community took form the day when
the group, which had been talking together and
studying the Bible, decided to reconstruct the* barraco
*of a widow with ten children and expecting the
eleventh. Her husband had been killed some days
earlier on the highway that passes not far from us.
So it was decided that one Sunday morning all the
volunteers would show up with saws, hammer and
nails, and axes at seven in the morning to work on
the widow's house. What happened was what has
been happening since human beings appeared on
earth.*

*Initially there was laziness or fatigue. A person
who has worked hard all week long, on an
impossible schedule, never wants to lose Sunday rest.
And so a certain number of the biblical circle were
not there at the hour agreed on. The rest waited for
them, in vain, all day long. No doubt each one had
a valid excuse.*

*And throughout there was the usual difficulty that
people have working together. Nobody wants to be*

[3] Church, Charism and Power, p. 9.

*ordered around by somebody else, especially when
the task is one of benevolence. 'I know how to build
a* barraco *at least as well as you do.' 'I don't need to
take orders from you.' Each one has a different idea
how to proceed. And a third part of the volunteer
army disappears into the wood on one pretext or
another. It looks very much like the story of
Gideon's army: the force that was to confront Midian
shrank from 20,000 to 300! It was with 300
courageous men, chosen by God, that Gideon
confronted the enemies of his people—a remnant
fighting against a much more powerful enemy
(Judges 7:1–8). It is the same way with base communities. In the case we describe, those who stuck it
out to the end at the widow's house, who overcame
the obstacles to action, still today, after six years,
make up the cadre of the community!*

   *. . . It is certain that prayer, the celebration of the
faith, biblical and theological study, and nourishment
by the sacraments are indispensable to gospel energy,
as we have insisted. But we must never forget that
only action can verify whether or not prayer is
authentic: 'Not those who say "Lord, Lord" . . .' (Mt
7:21). People can pray together for twenty years side
by side in the same church and never have a
disagreement. But on the day when they begin to act
together, everything starts to change. That is when
we see whether the charity that 'bears all things,
hopes all things, believes all things, endures all
things' (1 Cor 13:7) will win out over our egotism
and allow us to work together.*

   *That is the decisive moment when a base
community is born.*[4]

The next passage, from Uriel Molina, speaking about pre-
revolutionary Nicaragua, illustrates how deeply steeped in life the
liturgy was, and how powerful it became because of that. At the
same time we can see that protest without this dimension of worship
would have lacked depth and richness compared to what we have
here. It is in the combination of faith and life that the power lies.

[4] Grace and Power, pp. 99–100.

A Nicaraguan Good Friday

*Prayer was always an extremely important element in
the life of the community. We almost always prayed
in a communal way. Prayer came to be the sharing
of a social need, which was then offered to the Lord.
We held spiritual retreats for the leaders, but the
ordinary people expressed themselves best in the
great festivals of the liturgical year. In the Holy
Week celebrations, it was a matter of expressing,
through the Passion of Christ, the pain of a suffering
people. The wooden cross carried by the Nazarene
was covered with newspaper cuttings containing
reports of deaths and disappearances, or protests
about the violation of human rights. The young men
preached the Via Crucis in the streets, as they
denounced the atrocities committed under the
dictatorship of Somoza. The vigil of Holy Saturday
was also very well attended. There were no public
readings, but rather study-groups around bonfires. In
these, the meditation centred on three points: the
Hebrew Passover, the Passover of Jesus, and the
Passover of our people. We were greatly helped by
no. 5 in the Introduction to the Medellín statement:
'We cannot fail to hear the step of the Lord who
saves us, when we pass from less human conditions
to more human ones . . .' The ceremony ended with
a procession led by a cross of flowers, symbolising
the resurrection and the hope of our people.*[5]

BASE COMMUNITY IS ABOUT LOVE AND SHARING

'By this, all will know that you are my disciples, if you have love
for one another' (John 13:35). You cannot get much more basic
than that. In the last analysis we judge any Church movement—or
indeed any movement at all—by its fruits of love. There is no need
to explain that, we just know it to be true.

[5] Uriel Molina, *Concilium* 176, p. 6.

In this passage from *Revolution from the Heart*, an account of forming base communities in the Philippines, Niall O'Brien tells how this message of love and sharing, at the heart of the Christian community, really struck home for him:

The five-pointed star

He went to the board and drew a five-pointed star. He turned around and said to me: 'I don't mean to criticize you, Niall. When you started all those panimbahons *in the mountains and all over Negros, it was a good thing. It gave people a chance to worship which they did not have before . . . But in a way, don't feel hurt now, it might have done more harm than good, because implicit in that movement was the idea that if the people worship, then that's it. Oh, I know that's furthest from your mind, but that's the way our people take it. Prayer is cake. Once they have the cake they are no longer interested in more mundane foods. What you were establishing was worship services, not Christian communities. But it's communities of love and sharing which we are all about. Look at the early Christians.' And he flipped open the Acts of the Apostles, reading aloud as he wrote on the blackboard: 'And all who believed were together and had all things in common; and they sold their possessions and goods and distributed them to all, as any had need. There was not a needy person among them.'*

Then Peter returned to the star: 'Christian community is like this five-pointed star.' Opposite each point he wrote some words: (1) Sharing: time, treasure, talent; (2) Group decision-making; (3) No injustice; (4) Reconciliation; (5) Prayer together.

'Don't be shocked that I wrote prayer last. For too long we have put it so strongly first that the other essential parts of being a disciple have been lost. It must be there, but as a culmination, a celebration, a part of the whole, not itself the whole. I put sharing first because if we are sisters and brothers then we share. That is our "good news", our "evangelion": we are brothers and sisters.'

He paused for a moment and added: 'If we are not sisters and brothers then there is no God and we have nothing to say.'

He went on to explain the other points. Group decision: the people must share in decisions that affect them, not just the priest or the village captain or the local big man must be involved, but everyone . . . But by this time I was no longer listening because the first point had already gone home so deeply that everything was falling together for me in advance of his words.

There is something in the human mind which wants to simplify, to reduce a sentence, a book, a philosophy, a religion, to one word. As you go on in life you keep realizing that one word is inadequate because things are complex and there are depths within depths. Yet nothing can take away the power of that moment when you glimpse through the complexity and see the underlying unity, the simplicity: like a person looking into a very deep well who sees first the insects playing on top of the water; further down he sees some moss or jutting rocks in the growing darkness; but then there is a moment when the light is right and he catches sight of a shining object way down at the bottom of the well. I seemed to catch sight of that object: being a disciple of Jesus means sharing, means community. There is no Christianity without community, and conversely atheism is in the last analysis the refusal to share—and that holds no matter what religion I profess and even if I am a priest.

Back at the blackboard star Peter was saying: 'By "no injustice" I mean that we cannot have community between two groups, one of which has its foot on the other's neck. There must be an attempt not only at charity but at changing the very structures which almost force people to oppress each other. But then again, we are not only after cold justice, some sort of mathematical equality. We want to work toward reconciliation . . . a warmth, an intimacy, affection, love! And then we can pray together without it being a mockery. If this star represents a basic Christian community, then our

*immediate aim is to start basic Christian
communities.'
But how?*[6]

So much for theory, but the practice works too! Pablo Galdámez[7]
tells how the beginnings of base community led to a real sharing
among the people:

A big family

*Now we were a people. We were like a big family.
We were friends. The community meetings bound us
closer and closer together. The doors were open. We
said hello to one another, we went to one another's
houses. For the first time, this scattered people was
united. Gone were fear and embarrassment. We
shared everything, a cup of coffee, a glass of
water — and the quest. We'd learned to share out the
solution to our problems together.*[8]

Those who have learned to share with members of their own community, who they know, easily share also with those who they have
never seen, just as the early Christians sent donations, according to
their ability, to bring relief to those suffering famine in Judea (Acts
11:29).

An offering on the altar

*Some communities in Guatemala celebrated a Mass
of solidarity with the people of the Church of
Nicaragua, which is scarred by the destruction of
war. During the offertory, each one placed on the
altar his offering to be sent to this suffering Church.
A poor man placed on the altar a small plastic bag
containing just a handful of beans. He was already
returning to his place when he stopped. He looked*

[6] *Revolution from the Heart*, pp. 82–3.
[7] A pseudonym, because of the very dangerous situation in El Salvador
at the time he wrote the book.
[8] *Faith of a People*, p. 21.

back. Then he walked up to the altar once again,
took off his jacket, folded it carefully, affectionately,
and left it there with the other offerings . . . the
temperature that evening was 10°C.

Even those who have nothing find they can share something. Pedro Arrupe, the former General of the Jesuits, visited a shanty town, and said mass there. He reports what happened next.

The sunset

At the end a big fellow, whose fearful looks could
have inspired fear, told me: 'Come to my house, I
have something to honour you.' I remained
uncertain, not knowing whether I should accept or
not, but the priest who was accompanying me said:
'Go with him, father, the people are very good.' I
went to his house, which was a half-falling shack. He
made me sit down on a rickety chair. From where I
was seated the sun could be seen as it was setting.
The fellow said to me: 'Señor, you see how beautiful
it is!' And we remained silent for some minutes. The
sun disappeared. The man added: 'I did not know
how to thank you for all that you have done for us.
I have nothing to give you, but I thought you would
like to see this sunset. It pleased you, didn't it?
Good evening.' He then gave me his hand. As I was
leaving, I thought: 'I have met very few hearts that
are so kind.'[9]

BASE COMMUNITY IS ABOUT THE ULTIMATE LOVE – MARTYRDOM

One kind of love and sharing leads to another, until, on occasions, the point is reached of 'no greater love' — the point where you find yourself asked to give your life for your friends.

There have been many martyrs in recent Latin American history.

[9] Jean-Claude Dietsch, *Pedro Arrupe: itinéraire d'un jésuite*
(Le Centurion, Paris, 1982), p. 47.

In general we only hear of the few who are bishops or priests or sisters. But behind them there are hundreds of humble peasants and martyrs, who have given their lives freely because of the commitment the basic Christian communities have led them to.

Martyrdom is an important dimension to recall, because it jolts us out of too cosy an understanding of community. Belonging to a community is not necessarily something comforting. It can be supportive, but it can also invite us to a new stage of vulnerability, that we would have avoided if we had stayed back at the level just of personal spirituality.

In the martyrs of Latin America — and of the Philippines too — we have more than just a moving and edifying story. They make real in today's world a key element in the Christian Church, and one which had become almost a quaint relic of the distant past. The early Church was full of martyrs — Christians whose lives had been taken in very bloody and horrific ways, because of their faith. Jesus himself gave his life in such a way.

As Christianity became the accepted religion of the Roman Empire, martyrdom — as a regular happening — became a thing of the past. The truth of giving one's life for one's friends had to be found in metaphorical ways.

We are living now in a new age of Christian martyrs. Those who have given their lives may be on the other side of the world, but they are witnesses for the whole Church. It would be a mistake to think that this kind of Church commitment is not relevant for us in the first world, because we do not live under that kind of threat.

On the contrary, it is as though we are walking at the back of a demonstrating crowd, and those in the front are being shot down. We are all in the same demonstration — proclaiming our faith in Jesus and in the way of life he taught us. The martyrs are bearing the gunfire on behalf of us all. They are *our* martyrs too — martyrs of the Church.

They remind us that Christian commitment means giving our lives, and that giving our lives can sometimes mean precisely that.

This 1974 account shows how simple peasants in Bolivia, through their involvement in base communities, came to exercise love and sharing, right up to the giving of their lives.

In the Altiplano of Bolivia

*It is very encouraging to see the Christian spirit
which animates these pastoral workers. They are not
paid for their work, which constitutes a heavy
sacrifice on their part since they have to pay
themselves for their journey to the monthly reunion
and even for the books they use. They are fully
aware that their means of livelihood must be the
same as those of any peasant, namely work on the
land and raising cattle.*

*They try to get as much as possible from their
training, not so much in order to achieve a higher
cultural level for themselves as to be able to help
others more effectively.*

*There are wonderful examples of zeal and charity
among these people. For example, a catechist of
Compi inherited some land from his father but his
brother seized it from him, using violence. All his
friends advised him to take his brother to court,
since he was without any doubt in the right. On the
contrary, he brought his brother before the local
authorities, but only to surrender this land officially
to him and to forgive him. This man works his land
for three days of the week in order to provide for his
family and dedicates the other four to the work of
evangelization.*

*In Cullucachi another catechist managed to get the
cooperation of the rest of the community to build six
classrooms for the religious and professional training
of the local peasants. He paid out of his own pocket,
using three years' savings, for the roofing. Another
catechist sold his cattle in order to pay for the
building of a centre for the religious training of the
people in the neighbourhood.*

*Three years ago a catechist was murdered by
members of a fanatical sect. Two young men
immediately went to see the parish priest and offered
to replace him. At a meeting of catechists a few
months later I was told that the home of one of
these young men had been visited that week by men
of the same sect. One easily can imagine their aim,*

but fortunately he was not there. Later, he told the other catechists that he was determined to follow his vocation and would have been glad to lay down his life for Christ's sake. And so a large number of catechists lead their Christian life, simply and generously.[10]

Leonardo Boff reminds us that today's spirituality of martyrdom is a return to the spirituality of the early Church:

The spirituality of martyrdom

In Latin America, when a member of a base ecclesial community is imprisoned (as happens so often), the others care for the prisoner's family, seek legal assistance, and support and encourage the prisoner through visits and various other means, as was done in the early Church.

In order to survive in a world that does not appear able to be transformed, the communities combine commitment with prudence, risk measured with courage. They act against the forces of oppression without unnecessarily provoking them. They have created a spirituality of martyrdom, accepting persecution, defamation, imprisonment, and even death itself, for the one who truly follows Jesus Christ.[11]

Another passage from Boff contrasts this spirituality of martyrdom with a very different attitude that afflicts many in the Church's hierarchy today:

Success or failure not a problem for the Church

There is a great difference between the Church of the first three centuries and the later Church which rose to power. The primitive Church was prophetic;

[10] Carlos Palmés SJ, *Pro Mundi Vita*, 50 (1974), Appendix 3, pp. 78–9.
[11] *Church, Charism and Power*, p. 137.

*it joyfully suffered torture and courageously gave its
life through martyrdom. It did not care about
survival because it believed in the Lord's promise
that guaranteed it would not fail. Success or failure,
survival or extinction, was not a problem for the
Church; it was a problem for God. The bishops were
at the forefront, convincing their brothers and sisters
to die for the Lord. The later Church was
opportunistic; that it would not fail was a question
of prudence and compromise that allowed it to
survive in the midst of totalitarian regimes, at the
expense of gospel demands. The bishop in this later
Church does not freely walk in witness to his death;
rather, he pushes others, walking behind his flock
and often assisting in the death of its prophets,
fearful and reticent, calling for fidelity not to Christ
but to the institutional Church.* [12]

This report of persecution in pre-revolutionary Nicaragua shows
how closely united a basic Christian community can become when
one member is suffering with faith.

When they tortured David

*When they tortured David, he wrote me many
letters: 'My brother: I don't know whether it's day or
night. I am naked. A guard stood over me and
wounded my testicles. I am passing blood. Tell the
community that I am offering all my sufferings to
the Lord, for the sake of the New Humanity we
want to build.' I replied with phrases from biblical
texts strung together, and sent him the eucharist so
that in prison he might share communion with his
companions. Never was the prayer-life of the community so intense as during the imprisonment of
David. His sufferings confirmed the faith of many —
including my own . . . His words gave me courage at
those times when it seemed that we had lost all
hope.* [13]

[12] Church, Charism and Power, pp. 54–5.
[13] Uriel Molina, Concilium 176, pp. 7–8.

Next comes an extract which speaks of two martyrs from El Salvador, the young priest Octavio Ortiz, and the most famous martyr of all, Monsignor Oscar Romero. When I was in El Salvador I visited the site of Octavio's murder, and, of course, the tomb of Romero.

We begin here to understand what people mean when they say the base communities place more emphasis on discovering what it means to be a eucharistic community, than just on frequent celebrations of the sacrament.

The eucharist celebrated in life itself

Father Octavio Ortiz was meeting with some young people in the parish hall of Saint Anthony Abbott. Octavio was a simple man, a campesino, who had long devoted his life to our communities. He had already had much experience in 'giving his life'. Octavio's presence was like the life-giving rain that falls on a field of new corn. The evening before, he had reflected with the young people on Jesus' healing of the blind. (Jesus came to give sight to the blind. Now, who are the blind of El Salvador?) And in the dawn light of the twentieth, an army death squad marched in and murdered four youths and Octavio.

Octavio had had his first pastoral experience in the slums, with us. He had been ordained a priest in our community and had celebrated his first Mass with us. He was our great friend. We all felt close to him. And now he was celebrating his last Eucharist, his Last Supper. His blood mixed with the blood of his young friends and the blood of the whole people in the greatest offering he could give to God, the greatest proof of his love . . . Octavio's blood taught us that the Eucharist must be celebrated in life itself, and that its sacramental celebration has meaning only if those who share in it are giving the gift of their lives.

. . . By murdering Archbishop Romero, on March 24, 1980, the killers thought that they could stifle the voice of the people . . . And so he was murdered, while celebrating Mass, with a single bullet through the heart.

. . . Now Oscar Arnulfo Romero is a shining signal to

the church universal in these times of struggle and hope. In our archbishop, God has taken sides with the poor in history, has taken up the cause of the people who go in quest of their liberation, has taken up the cause of the church that has committed itself to their struggle. Since the death of the shepherd every day is Good Friday for the flock, this people of priests, with blood on their vestments every day of the year, offer up to God a pleasing sacrifice for the world's redemption.[14]

Reminding us that martyrdom is not reserved to Latin America, we have next a story of two martyrs from the Philippines:

The passion-play Christ

In the barrio *of Tan-Awan on Easter Monday morning two of the Christian community leaders disappeared — Alex Garsales and Herman Muleta. Both had been leaders in the Christian community, both had had conflicts with the municipal authorities, and both had taken part in the just-finished Easter ceremonies. In fact Alex had played the part of Christ in the Passion play on Good Friday, and he had used the occasion to make a personal statement of faith. We still have it:*

> *My brothers: I, Alexander Garsales, of* barrio *Tan-Awan, do promise to be faithful, to continue teaching the people. I offer myself to defend the poor and oppressed, to stand for my brothers and sisters who are falsely condemned. I offer my life so that peace will prevail in this place of Tan-Awan . . . And I will bear all sufferings so that you, leaders, will not be cowed by threats. I have experienced many sufferings, yet I was not shaken nor discouraged. You made me Christ whom we are now celebrating and all should stand for the truth, as Christ did in the past, so that everyone will have faith.*

[14] Faith of a People, pp. 86–8.

> *Looking at this last testament of Alex Garsales I realize how the theology we had grown into over the years had penetrated all through our communities. We were preaching it, but they were doing it with their lives.*[15]

The last word goes to one of the martyrs, Luis Espinal, a Jesuit who was tortured and then killed in Bolivia on 21 March 1980. The martyrdom of Luis made a deep impression on my family, because he had been a friend of my husband some twenty years earlier, in his native Spain.

We are candles

> *We are candles that only have meaning if we are burning, for only then do we serve our purpose of being light. Free us from the cowardly prudence that makes us avoid sacrifice and look only for security. Losing one's life should not be accompanied by pompous or dramatic gestures. Life is to be given simply, without fanfare, like a waterfall, like a mother nursing her child, like the humble sweat of the sower of seed. Train us, Lord, and send us out to do the impossible, because behind the impossible is your grace and your presence; we cannot fall into the abyss. The future is an enigma; our journey leads us through the fog; but we want to go on giving ourselves because you are waiting there in the night, in a thousand human eyes brimming over with tears.*[16]

BASE COMMUNITY IS ABOUT MISSION

Mission or Maintenance? asks Michael Winter, in the famous title of his book. Not surprisingly he sees base communities as a way of moving to a more mission-orientated Church.

[15] Niall O'Brien, *Revolution from the Heart*, p. 165.
[16] *A New Way of Being Church: Interviews and Testimonies from Latin America Press*, p. 36.

A basic ecclesial community does not ultimately exist for the sake of its own members: it exists to spread the Gospel, to take the good news to the poor, to be a local base for the mission of the Church. This is another aspect of the basics of Christianity which, like martyrdom, broadens its horizons and stops it becoming a cosy group.

It has been found in practice that this is not just a high-sounding theory beyond the capabilities of uneducated laity, but it really works. An agricultural community, for example, is often more effectively evangelized by other agricultural workers than by people coming from a different cultural and intellectual background.

José Marins stresses the importance of the 'mission' dimension in a base community. When people begin to tread on each other's toes in a community, he says, it is time to ask if we have forgotten about mission. People become united in working on something important together.

This is another way into understanding why a basic Christian community is not just formed out of a group of friends. A basic Christian community, says Marins' colleague Carolee Chanona, is not necessarily a homogeneous group: the community is in the goal, or the mission, that brings us together.

There are two essential dynamics of the human heart, continues Marins (he and Carolee customarily speak in alternation like this, adding to each other's words). On the one hand there is the movement towards building community; on the other, the movement that reaches out, towards mission. The pastoral task is to balance the two.

The tension between the two, adds Carolee, is a healthy tension — the tension between Peter and Paul — and it will always be with us. We need both dynamics, so that we can be both a missionary community, and a communitarian mission.

'Mission' may sound a grand word, but the reality of it is something very simple, as this first-hand account of a Nicaraguan woman testifies.

The parish here mentioned — St Paul the Apostle (San Pablo Apóstol) in Managua — was probably the first place in Nicaragua to form base communities. The parish was created in 1966 to be a pilot project for pastoral work in the diocese, and over the next few years it was much helped by the example of San Miguelito in Panama, which had already developed base communities and was a great influence on many other parishes in the Central American region. There were several missionary visits between San Miguelito and San Pablo Apóstol. By 1968 many other places in Nicaragua were looking to the San Pablo Apóstol for missionary help in their formation of base communities.[17]

A commitment in the parish of St Paul the Apostle

I shall begin by giving a brief account of how I came to join a Christian community away back about 1970. A neighbour invited me to go to a meeting with a Spanish priest who had newly arrived into the parish of St Paul the Apostle — the neighbourhood of Ducalí, to which I belong, forms part of this parish. I went to the meeting and I met this nice-looking young priest who treated us as equals; we discussed things of general interest and we were very impressed and keen to go to the next meeting. Soon, we began to study a short course of Initiation into the Christian Life and at the end of the course we met at a retreat house. This was a marvellous meeting and one that I shall never forget; there was one particular experience which I have special reason for remembering — the welcome that they gave us in one small church. When the bus that brought us there came to a halt, the doorway of the church was all joy, congratulations and affectionate greetings. A poor lady embraced me happily and congratulated me. They looked on us as if we had come from heaven and in fact I now think that we had just come from talking with God. And that is when I made my commitment. We just had to show all these people that we had come ready for work, that the seed had fallen on good ground and that the strength of their moral support would produce good fruit.[18]

Leonardo Boff gives us here a theological basis for the missionary activity of the basic ecclesial community.

[17] See Félix Jiménez, 'La parroquia San Pablo, germen de las comunidades de base en Nicaragua' in Girardi and others (eds), *Nicaragua, Trinchera Teologica*.

[18] Leonor Tellería, *Concilium* 176, pp. 67–8.

The entire community is apostolic

The difficulty with the current understanding of apostolic succession arose when the original twelve apostles were considered individually. The symbolic meaning of the number 'twelve' as a designation of the messianic community (the new Israel), and its collegiality, was lost. The fact is that the apostles were not sent out individually; it was the group, the collegium, *the community of the Twelve, that is, the first small* ecclesia *gathered around Jesus, that was sent out. As such, it is the entire community that is apostolic, and not only certain holders of sacred power.*

The base ecclesial communities recover this original meaning of apostolicity inasmuch as the community, as community, senses itself as sent out to be the carrier of the orthodox doctrine of faith, sharing the various services brought forth by the Spirit, living an apostolic life through the following of Jesus, his attitudes, his message, and the hope for the Kingdom that has been deposited in the heart of the person of faith. Apostolic succession is not limited to hierarchical function, which divides the community. Everyone is a bearer of the teachings of Jesus Christ and all share in the three basic tasks: to give witness, to sanctify, and to be responsible for the unity and life of the community.[19]

BASE COMMUNITY IS ABOUT READING THE BIBLE CONTEXTUALLY

It is well known that base communities read and discuss the Bible. Even if the people are illiterate they will listen attentively while maybe the only literate member among them stumblingly reads it out. For Catholics, who are notoriously ignorant of the Bible, this has been an important new departure, and a real return to the basics of Christianity.

It is appropriate that the base communities should read the

[19] *Church, Charism and Power*, p. 123.

Bible, because the Bible is the history of the community of God—and so it is their history too. The book is sacred: in liturgies it is sometimes held aloft with great honour and applause—it was surrounded by flaming torches at the Seventh Interecclesial Assembly of CEBs in Brazil. But 'it is not only the book that is sacred', says José Marins, 'the community is sacred, life is sacred.'

Just as important as reading the Bible is what they do with it. The communities read the scriptures contextually. Life gives a context to understanding the message of the Bible, and the Bible gives a context to understanding the message of life. And so the biblical texts seem to come alive to these poor communities, in a way that baffles learned intellectuals. Their interpretations are often so fresh that we might call them 'lateral thinking'.

The people's lack of learning—which we might think a disadvantage—is more than balanced by the simple directness with which the biblical message seems to speak to them in their immediate circumstances of need. It is as though their eyes are opened and their ears unstopped by their very poverty, to see and hear what the 'good news to the poor' (Luke 4:18) is all about. And so they go right to the heart of the matter and make apposite and direct applications to their everyday life. This way of reading the Bible is sometimes called 'contextual reading'.

Carlos Mesters—himself a proficient biblical scholar, but one who has devoted his life to popular education among the biblical circles and base communities of Brazil—sees the Bible as really coming alive when three elements are present. First of course there must be the text itself. Then there is the 'con-text', which is the community discussing it as community, and not just as a group of individuals. Thirdly you need the 'pre-text', which is the real life situation of the people that comes before their reading of the Bible and places it in a vivid perspective in their lives.[20]

Uriel Molina's observation here has been made by countless others who have heard the scriptural interpretations coming out of the base communities.

---

[20] See Carlos Mesters, 'The Bible in Christian Communities' in Sergio Torres and John Eagleson (eds), *The Challenge of Basic Christian Communities* (Orbis, 1981).

A sixth sense

*Anyone who has practical experience of a basic
community recognizes immediately that the poor
have a sort of sixth sense which enables them to
grasp the message of the Bible. The poor know that
the Bible speaks for them, so that, when they read a
passage carefully, they immediately begin to give
very colourful and eloquent expression to it.* [21]

Building on the same observation, Leonardo Boff points out that
this method of biblical analysis is surprisingly similar to the tradition of exegesis found among the early fathers of the Church (and
which is very different from modern scripture scholarship).

Close to the exegesis of the Fathers

*The Gospel is shared in absolute freedom in the base
ecclesial community. Everyone is given the chance to
speak and to give their opinion about a given fact or
situation. Surprisingly, the popular exegesis of the
community comes very close to the ancient exegesis
of the fathers of the Church. It is an exegesis that
goes beyond the words and captures the living,
spiritual meaning of the text.* [22]

Carlos Mesters gives an example of the people's insights:

Heeding the cries of the people

*The common people are discovering things in the
Bible that other readers don't find. At one session
we were reading the following text: 'I have heard the
cries of my people.' A woman who worked in a
factory offered this commentary: 'The Bible does not
say that God has heard the praying of the people. It
says that God has heard the cries of his people. I
don't mean that people shouldn't pray. I mean that*

[21] Concilium 176, p. 5.
[22] Church, Charism and Power, p. 127.

*people should imitate God. Very often we work to
get people to go to church and pray first; and only
then will we pay heed to their cries.' You just won't
find that sort of interpretation in books.*[23]

Here is an interpretation with a particular message for Europeans.

Latin America has good news for Europe

*In April 1981, living in forced exile in Europe, I
received a visit from my great friend Lito. First we
just talked, a long while. Then we began to
meditate on Mary's visit to Elizabeth before the
coming of the Saviour.*

   *Lito's visit gave me the hope and joy that
Elizabeth must have felt when Mary came to see her.
Lito compared Europe to the mother of the
forerunner. He said that he and I, filled with the
living experiences of the Salvadorean people, were a
sign, as Mary was to Elizabeth. Latin America, he
said, was pregnant, heavy with the Lord. Pregnant
with hope, in labour with the new human being.
Latin America had good news for Europe.*[24]

And here, in a different image, is another message for the first
world, brought back this time by Derek Winter, a Baptist from the
former British Council of Churches, who attended one of the big
Interecclesial Assemblies of base communities in Brazil.

Good seed to plant in the first world

*We celebrated the Bible as the book that speaks
more powerfully than any other to a people who are
homeless in the land where they were born, and who
find in its stories and images the most natural way to
describe their own life. The story of Abraham and
Sara and their wandering is the story of Genesio and*

[23] In Torres and Eagleson (eds), *The Challenge of Basic Christian
Communities*, p. 207.
[24] *Faith of a People*, p. xvii.

*Rosa, migrant farm workers. The man who fell
among thieves is the peasant attacked by the hired
gunman; the land-owner and the government official
pass by on the other side but the local Christian
community take his part. Good news becomes good
reality. . . . 'I've got it' said one woman I talked
with, in a community in the sticks of Bahia
explaining my job: 'You've come looking for the
good seed that you can plant back in your own
country.'*[25]

Next we have a brief but memorable anecdote brought back by Ian
Fraser from one of his trips.

The image of God

*An Indian group were examining what it meant that
they were all made in the image of God. It suddenly
struck them that this was news applicable to their
present situation. 'It means that we are the equal of
the landlord!' said the men; 'and that we are the
equal of you' said the women.*[26]

I was struck by this witness of a lay missionary, Jill Marshall, about
the way the scriptures spoke to her, as a US citizen, when inter-
preted by the members of the Adolfo Reyes base community. I
quote from a recorded conversation I had with her in Managua.

Land is life here

*I think the prophets are speaking to us. The whole
prophetic tradition is a tradition that we really need
to listen to. And I see the third-world, poor
Christians are really serving that function for us —
that we need to look at the way that we are living,
and look at our values. And I think they are the
ones who can help us to do that because of the*

---

[25] Report by Derek Winter on the Sixth Interecclesial Assembly of CEBs,
held at Trindade, Goiania, 21–25 July 1986.
[26] Report by Ian Fraser on 1986 visit to Central America, Scottish
Churches House, Dunblane.

whole, global connection now of our wealth and their poverty.

Theologically for me the most valuable thing is reading scripture in this community, in a community that is so much closer in their life style, and their values too, to Palestine of two thousand years ago. To read the Old Testament in an agrarian culture — it comes alive in a way that it cannot possibly in the States. (Because it is still an agrarian culture, even in the city, because these people come from the campo so that way of life and those values are still present.)

So when you read about each man sitting under his own fig tree and having his own little piece of land, that is very real to these folks. Land, which means nothing to us in the States except an investment, land is life here. Deyzy said, about how people were organized in this barrio *during the revolution: 'people wanted their piece of land'. All the symbols and the language and all of that, it's so real here.*

Finally, I recall what for me was a privileged moment in my journey to Nicaragua in January 1989, when I experienced what contextual reading of the scriptures was all about.

Forgive them, for they know not what they do

I was in Jinotega, high in the mountains, an area where there had been much fighting in the war with the Contras. In fact on the journey up the mountain our landrover had been stopped by a young woman: she wanted to tell us about the death of some friends from a Contra bomb that very week.

We were now in a hall filled with about forty peasant women members of the local Committee of Mothers of Heroes and Martyrs. The women were tiny, and very brown-skinned, and many of them looked as though they must have Indian blood in them. There was one man, and a few children stood around. Then there were the two catechists — one from Managua, and the other from a town a little further down the mountain-side, Matagalpa, where the Mothers' Committee was very well-organized and active.

The catechist from Managua was showing them a slide of a conventional, Spanish-style crucifix — a very bloody portrayal — and she was asking simple questions about what they were seeing. At first the answers came slowly. Then one woman began to speak more fluently, 'It shows Jesus shedding his blood for us', she was saying, and then she suddenly became very agitated and burst into tears: 'And that is what my son did — he shed his blood for us. He fought to free us from the Contras, and they killed him. He shed his blood like Jesus, and he is dead, and I don't know how to go on living. I pray that God may help me to forgive his assassins, but I find it so hard . . .'

Another woman went to fetch her a glass of water, and the catechist from Matagalpa — who had also lost a son in the war — gently spoke. 'On the cross Jesus said "Father, forgive them, for they know not what they do". That is our example. We have to say with Jesus, about the death of our sons, "Father, forgive them, for they know not what they do".'

BASE COMMUNITY IS ABOUT READING CHURCH TRADITION CONTEXTUALLY

What is less often noticed, is that base communities approach the devotional language of the Church with just the same freshness as they do the scriptures. In this way they are constantly finding new applications for traditional concepts, that might otherwise lie gathering dust, neglected as outdated, and so the Church's tradition, far from being pushed aside as a thing of the past, swims into new and vivid perspective.

This constant exploration of new interpretations and new applications is probably what Cardinal Ratzinger had in mind when he criticized liberation theologians for continuing 'to use a great deal of the Church's classical, ascetical and dogmatic language while changing its significance'.[27] However, *changing* its significance is not the same thing as *rediscovering* its significance through new, contemporary applications.

We have already seen, on p. 58 above, an example of this, in the new depth of eucharistic understanding that comes through the experience of martyrdom. We can also point to the way the people from the base communities recognize modern saints, canonizing their heroes and martyrs by popular usage, without waiting for any official process in Rome. They now talk about St Romero of the Americas, that is, Archbishop Oscar Romero of San Salvador, their great advocate and friend, who was shot while saying mass in 1980. Here are a couple more examples of this vivid, modern rediscovery of traditional concepts.

In this example given by Carlos Mesters, we can notice just the same approach to interpreting a papal encyclical as the people would use in interpreting scripture:

Spiritual things, such as food for the people

The common people are giving us a clearer picture of concepts that have been excessively spiritualized. Let me give just one example. Some time ago Pope Paul VI delivered an address in which he warned priests not to become overly preoccupied with material things. He urged them to show greater concern for spiritual things. One farmworker in Goiás had this comment: 'Yes, the pope is quite right. Many priests concern themselves only with material things, such as building a church or decorating it. They forget spiritual things, such as food for the people!'

This is what the people are doing with such notions as grace, salvation, sin, and so forth. They are dusting them off and showing us that these notions have to do with solid, concrete realities of life.[28]

[27] Joseph Cardinal Ratzinger with Vittorio Messori, *The Ratzinger Report* (Ignatius Press, 1985), p. 176. The quotation comes from a 'private' document that is believed to have been written by Ratzinger, who is Prefect of the Sacred Congregation for the Doctrine of the Faith.
[28] Torres and Eagleson (eds), *The Challenge of Basic Christian Communities*, p. 209.

We have now another extract from Derek Winter's report on the Sixth Interecclesial Assembly of CEBs in Brazil. As we read through it we can pick out a number of traditional features, like the candlelit procession and the use of relics — not to mention the 'old-fashioned revival meeting' — now given contemporary meaning. The biblical theme of the promised land also acquires a new significance for today.

Worship at the Sixth Interecclesial Assembly

We celebrated in drama, symbol and song. Worship was at the heart of the Encontro, and do these people know how to celebrate! At times during the singing, you might have mistaken it for an old fashioned revival meeting — until you listened to what they *were singing! But even more impressive was the use of symbol and imagery. A candlelit procession on the first night from the stadium, where the main meetings were held, up to the basilica on the hill above us, engendered a sense of unity in the pilgrimage in which everyone was engaged. During a service that celebrated the martyrs, a large cross was carried solemnly through the assembly. Having been placed in position at the rostrum, it was then festooned with the modern equivalent of the relics of the martyrs, including the bloodstained shirt that Padre Josimo[29] had been wearing at the time of his murder in May. At the opening ceremony, each Regional Group brought a handful of earth to add to a bowl, which reappeared at the final Eucharist to symbolise the new earth that God's people are looking for. It was as if to say: 'This we offer to God along with the bread and wine in the faith that just as he takes them and transforms them, so this Brazilian soil will in his*

---

[29] Josimo Moraes Tavares, martyr for the cause of the landless, was represented at the Assembly by his mother. The final Letter referred to her in the context of traditional Marian devotion, as follows: 'We feel deeply moved at the presence of Dona Olinda, mother of Father Josimo, who brings to mind the courageous figure of Our Lady of Sorrows and of all the mothers of our martyr-people.'

transforming power become genuinely the land of God and the land of Brothers.'[30]

BASE COMMUNITY IS ABOUT CELEBRATION AND SYMBOL

That last passage about the Sixth Interecclesial Assembly introduces a further theme that we cannot overlook, and that is the base communities' tremendous ability to celebrate, and to celebrate particularly with the use of symbol.

Celebration — the last item on the pastoral circle — brings spice to the whole Christian process of bringing together faith and life. It brings also depth, and joy, and sheer relaxation.

Symbol in celebration enables the Christian message to reach parts that purely verbal language can never reach. It speaks to us in ways that can never be confined to words. That makes symbol a very important medium of communication for people who are not so articulate, and maybe not literate. But it is not only those people who need symbol: wordy intellectuals have great need of symbol, precisely because that is the side of their personalities that has tended to be underdeveloped.

Modern Catholics have a great need to use symbol in their celebrations, because in many places there has been a loss of symbolic communication since the mass went into the vernacular (the language of the country). Before the reforms, people would worship on their knees, burying their heads in their hands out of reverence, breathing in the smell of incense, looking up at an altar adorned with gold and lace, and far away up front there would be the blessed mumble of the mass in a mystically foreign language. Many found a sense of mystery there, even if they did not understand a word.

Now that the words have become so important, we have tended (in many parts of the world) to fall into the error of replacing symbolic language with verbal language entirely. From beginning to end we have a barrage of words, and after a while we cannot take them in.

Of course the base communities are the first to rejoice about having the mass in the vernacular. But rather than letting the words flow over them — as though they might just as well be in Latin — the base communities dwell on scripture, rereading it and having

[30] See note 25 above.

everyone talk about it together, so that its message is not lost and everyone is made to think. We need to learn from them how to reap value from the verbal messages of celebration.

But the base communities also have something very important to teach us in their use of symbol. They know how to communicate the word of God in languages other than words, in music and mime and imagery. There are innumerable examples of this, but here we can recall just a handful of symbols that have been used effectively.

We have already used a couple of Derek Winter's recollections of the Sixth Interecclesial Assembly of CEBs in Brazil, but here are a couple of symbols from my memories of the Seventh Assembly, which I attended in July 1989 in Duque de Caxias.

Symbol at the Seventh Interecclesial Assembly

The most important and creative liturgies of this Assembly were ecumenical, including the three-and-three-quarter-hour opening ceremony, attended by 5,000 people, and held in the open air of a sports stadium. Each Latin American country made its own presentation with the use of symbols. Haiti, for example—hailed as the poorest country in Latin America, and one where base communities are particularly booming—brought a huge load of cocoa that needed four people to carry it: it represented the burden that their people bear. During a reading of the creed a group of children released some pigeons, which flew and soared above us.

Then those who had been present at the First Assembly of Basic Ecclesial Communities at Vitória in 1975—a gathering of only about 70 people— threw handfuls of seeds into the crowd to show how small beginnings had reaped a mighty harvest. We all scrabbled around the ground at our feet, and everyone managed to find at least two or three seeds or little dried fragments of maize. We were acting out what had really happened to us: each of us, through one route or another, had picked up the fertile seed of basic Christian community from that small and early beginning. And the seed had grown in us to the point that some of us had crossed the world to be present at that Assembly. What a precious seed we knew it to be!

An hour or so later, when darkness had already fallen, we reached the climax—the reading of the Word of God. I will never forget the excitement of that moment, when a huge open Bible was carried in, held high above the head, and flanked by seven flaming torches and seven palm branches. As it came to the centre of the platform, it was greeted with a triumphantly declaimed speech of praise: here was the Bible that gives life and hope to the communities of God's people. I have never known the scriptures greeted with such enthusiasm.

Then there was the music: the crowd undulated with rows of singing, swaying people, each delegate with a little coloured flag of a Latin American country to wave in the air, and a couple of sticks (symbolising the wooden huts of the favelas*) to clap in rhythm with the music. The favourite hymns rang out—which were to become so familiar over the next five days: 'We are a new people, living in unity, the seed of a new nation, Eh, eh!' 'Awake America, the hour has come to rise up!'*

Finally the local bishop, Dom Mauro Morelli, drew our attention through the evening blackness to a distant light of the famous, towering statue of Christ the Redeemer in Rio, visible even at this distance. 'His left hand is pointing over here, towards Duque de Caxias', he said. Duque de Caxias is considered one of the most violent areas in the world, and within Brazil it has the reputation of being the national cess-pit, for its street murders, drugs and prostitution. But Christ the Redeemer was telling us, 'That is where my heart is.' [31]

It is not only in huge congresses of thousands of people that we can experience powerful liturgies and expressive symbols. Here is an example from a much smaller and more modest gathering I attended

---

[31] Adapted from my articles in *The Tablet* (5 August 1989) and *Alpha* (17 August 1989).

in El Salvador. Present were around seventy base community representatives, mostly from very poor, rural communities which had known terrible violence and bloodshed.

Symbols of sin

In our small groups we were asked to spend the morning dwelling on the idea of sin. We were to read Ephesians 4:22–24, about getting rid of our old self, with its desires and deceits and corruption, and putting on a new self, which was upright and holy and in God's likeness. We were asked to consider what fault we have shown in our commitment to the oppressed, and how we could overcome this fault. Finally we were to prepare a symbol or socio-drama to show to the rest of the gathering.

Three symbols that spoke effectively were all little mimes. In one, a peasant struggled to carry a heavy stone, which was weighing him down. The stone, we were told, was the fear of persecution, which could often become a disabling weight to impede community work. Sin here was fear. And I was struck shortly after this by something said to me by a priest who worked with the communities: 'These people are not concerned about danger, they are concerned about being faithful.'

The second symbol showed someone holding up a branch of green leaves. Nearby were two twigs that had become detached from the tree. One was beginning to wilt. The other was quite dead. Sin here was breaking away from Christ the vine.

Thirdly a couple stepped forward with their arms linked, each carrying a long stick. On the ground were two oranges, just out of reach. With their sticks each tried to gather in an orange, stretching as far as the partner would permit—who was stretching in the opposite direction. They failed to reach them. Then another couple stepped forward with their arms linked. Instead of pulling in opposite directions, they both turned together, first to collect the orange on the left, then the orange on the right. This time it was easy. The message this time was that sin was

*individualism, but by working together we can
achieve goals that are impossible alone.*

You do not have to be a Latin American to use symbol effectively!
Here is a small but vivid example from a base community workshop
in England.

The parable of the needle

*All through the workshop a woman had sat quietly,
sewing a little tapestry on her knee. She had been a
peaceful presence, saying little, but absorbing all
that had been going on. Now the time came for her
group to introduce the next session.*

*The woman stepped forward. 'A needle', she
began, holding one up, 'has two ends. One end is
for pushing, and the other for pulling. If you push
it too hard, you will prick your finger, which will
bleed. If you pull it too hard, you will strain the
thread, which will break. We must push, and pull,
but do so gently, to keep both people and process
intact.' Then she sat down, her message complete.*

3

Base community is about the base of society—the poor

After exploring the meaning of 'the basic cell of the Church' and 'the basics of Christianity', we come now to the third mark of the base community: 'basic ecclesial community is about the base of society'. Another way of talking about this is through the well-publicized and much-discussed phrase 'preferential option for the poor'. But what does 'option for the poor' mean?

OPTION FOR THE POOR IS A CONSTITUTIVE ELEMENT OF THE GOSPEL

This principle is often misunderstood, for some people try to claim that because 'preferential option for the poor' contains the word 'option', therefore it is optional. Rather, 'option' means choice, and the 'preferential option for the poor' is the preferred choice of the Church as a whole, in fidelity to the priorities of Jesus himself, who came 'to preach good news to the poor' (Luke 4:18).

The option for the poor is a way in which the Church makes its own the concerns of God: 'I have seen the affliction of my people who are in Egypt, and have heard their cry because of their taskmasters; I know their sufferings, and I have come

77

down to deliver them' (Exodus 3: 7–8).

'Option for the poor' has other names: the Church of England sometimes speaks of 'bias to the poor'; the Vatican—shunning the terminology of liberation theology—uses the phrase 'love of preference for the poor'. But the concept is the same.

After the Second Vatican Council it was agreed that synods of bishops would meet regularly in Rome, and the third of these synods (in 1971) produced a document called *Justice in the World*. The following section includes the famous phrase about justice being 'a constitutive dimension of the preaching of the gospel'. The term 'justice' is so regularly linked with the idea of option for the poor that we can say the two concepts are inseparable.[1]

In other words, the synod is saying precisely that the preferential option for the poor is *not* optional.

Justice as a constitutive dimension

Listening to the cry of those who suffer violence and are oppressed by unjust systems and structures, and hearing the appeal of a world that by its perversity contradicts the plan of its creator, we have shared our awareness of the Church's vocation to be present in the heart of the world by proclaiming the good news to the poor, freedom to the oppressed, and joy to the afflicted. The hopes and forces which are moving the world in its very foundations are not foreign to the dynamism of the gospel, which through the power of the Holy Spirit frees people from personal sin and from its consequences in social life.

The uncertainty of history and the painful convergences in the ascending path of the human community direct us to sacred history; there God has revealed himself to us, and makes known to us, as it is brought progressively to realization, his plan of liberation and salvation which is once and for all fulfilled in the paschal mystery of Christ. Action on behalf of justice and participation in the transformation of the world fully appear to us as a constitutive dimension of the preaching of the

[1] See also **justice** and **option for the poor** in Appendix 1.

> *gospel, or, in other words, of the Church's mission*
> *for the redemption of the human race and its*
> *liberation from every oppressive situation.*[2]

In reply to those who claim that the Church should steer clear of politics, the Latin American Bishops' Conference meeting at Puebla[3] in 1979 pointed out that this approach usually amounts to what is in effect a highly political agenda, that is, to promote the political *status quo*. Particularly in situations where the *status quo* is leading to suffering and death on a massive scale, this supposedly 'a-political' presentation of the gospel message is a hideous distortion of the gospel.

It is very widely believed that the fundamentalist Protestant sects which are sweeping through Latin America, and which preach precisely such an 'a-political' gospel (in effect, 'God made rich and poor, so let's accept our place in society'), are funded and promoted by US sources with a highly political agenda — to oppose socialism.

Complicity with the established order

> *There is a manipulation of the Church that may*
> *derive from Christians themselves, and even from*
> *priests and religious, when they proclaim a Gospel*
> *devoid of economic, social, cultural and political*
> *implications. In practice, this mutilation comes down*
> *to a kind of complicity with the established order,*
> *however unwitting.*[4]

The 'father of liberation theology', Gustavo Gutiérrez, expressed the centrality of the poor for all Christians, in an address given at Worth Abbey, in prosperous south-east England. I have retained the appealing style of his unscripted delivery, making only minor corrections to his English.

---

[2] *Justice in the World*, 5–6; found in Walsh and Davies (see Bibliography).
[3] For **Puebla** see Appendix 1.
[4] Puebla Final Document, *Evangelization, Liberation and Human Promotion*, 5.6, (558).

Option for the poor not a third-world issue

People tell me: well, I understand you, you speak so strongly about poverty because you are Latin American. My answer is always the same: please don't understand me so quickly. Because my first reason for speaking about the poor is not because I am Latin American — that is my second reason. My first reason is because I am Christian. And I try to be Christian, I try to believe in the God of Jesus Christ. That is my first reason. It is not the social analysis (though it is very helpful really). It is not human compassion (though very important as well). My main reason for being committed to the poor is because I try to believe in the God of Jesus Christ. And if we have the same God, it is your duty as well.

It is not a Latin American question, it is not a third-world issue, it is a Christian question. And when we say — in the beginning in the Latin American framework (now it is more universal as an expression) — 'preferential option for the poor', it is not only good for people living in the poor countries. It is a challenge for all Christians. The ways to be committed to the poor and to really practise this preference, certainly they will be different. But this requirement I think is good and important for all Christians.[5]

The following story, from the journeys of José Marins, Carolee Chanona and Teolide Trevisan, illustrates the dangers of a spiritualized vision of the faith that cuts us off from the real and urgent problems of the world. The point of the story is not to reject the validity of the contemplative vocation, but to nudge us into realizing how we can manipulate the search for God into becoming an easy way out and a form of blindness.

Option for the poor, as a choice of the entire Church, can be expressed in different ways by different people in their different callings. Contemplatives, too, can live an option for the poor, if their life of prayer reflects an awareness of 'the beggar at the gate'.

The story comes from Cagayan de Oro in the Philippines:

[5] 5 May 1989.

From orphanage to convent

*After the course was over we went out to get to
know the various works and projects of the Church
in that area. We visited first a particular orphanage
which is also a house of young workers and a refuge
for people suffering from different diseases,
especially the blind.*

*We were moved as we went in by a blind woman
who was singing with the group, unaware of the
grotesque appearance of her deformed face.
Sad-looking children did not smile once. Teo and
Carolee took the children in their arms. They were
ecstatic, as if never in their life they had received the
least gesture of love. Neither one understood the
other's language. Few of them could say a word
outside of their dialect. To be with these people,
who understood us only through gestures of
friendship, through the expression of sympathy, was
the most profitable and important thing we did
during our stay in the city. We spent our time with
the poor and the despised, with the little ones, those
who could not offer reflections on anything, only
their own life, and that was no small thing!*

*We went from there, from that little city of those
who are poor and in pain, where the healthy help
the sick and one solitary nun is responsible for
everything and everyone without other help.*

*We went up a little hill. The geographical and
human panorama changed completely. Here was an
immense property which, after passing through a
security gate/checkpoint, you enter as though going
into an earthly paradise of order, cleanliness, beauty
and spaciousness, with colourful gardens and
perfumed flowers. There was an elegant building for
the church and convent. Thirty or forty nuns seek
here their sanctification in contemplation and in
painstaking care of their house. Some sell sweets and
religious trinkets to visitors to give economic
assistance for the upkeep of the house, so they say.*

*We looked up at it and were lost for words. A
little more than 500 metres away — in dirt, hardship,
misery, pain, the terrible struggle for life, the need*

*for love, the lack of the barest necessities for life of
any dignity — is just one sister, overburdened with
responsibilities and urgent tasks, tired, exhausted,
and paradoxically happy.*

*From there we went home. Really we had no
desire to visit further nor to learn other ways of
sanctification.*[6]

OPTION FOR THE POOR IS ABOUT CAUSES, NOT JUST CONSEQUENCES

Sooner or later everyone who works with the desperately poor seems
to come to the same conclusion: what point is there sticking a
plaster (or a band-aid) onto a wound if you do not also do
something about the aggravation that is causing the wound? What
point in wiping the fevered brows of those with typhoid, if you do
not inoculate their companions against catching the disease? What
point in visiting those sick with malaria, if you do not educate the
local community to avoid breeding grounds for mosquitoes? What
point in sending food aid, if you do not help the local people to
sow seed for next season? What point in collecting donations from
the first world to send abroad, if you do not also fund first-world
development education, to inform people about the international
economic causes of poverty and the ways of working for change?

It is because of the need to attend to causes that CAFOD had
adopted as one of its fundamental criteria in deciding how to spend
its money the following principle: 'The project should be concerned
with the causes as well as the conditions of poverty, hunger, disease,
ignorance and suffering.'

Again we have an extract from *Faith of a People*, recording the
point at which the community became acutely aware that they must
attend to causes, and not just consequences. (This passage follows
directly on from the paragraph quoted on p. 52 above.)

---

[6] *¿Salir o Quedarse?*, pp. 39–40.

Not irresponsibility but poverty

*We'd learned to search out the solution to our
problems together. There had been so many who
had had no time to reflect on them and try to find a
remedy.*

*Carlitos taught us that sickness wasn't the result
of irresponsibility. Sickness came from unsanitary
conditions. And unsanitary conditions were the result
of poverty. We also discovered that children's
sicknesses were almost always due to malnutrition.
And we learned that children weren't malnourished
because their mothers were irresponsible. They were
malnourished because their mothers were poor.*

*Carlitos was five years old. He had no toilet in his
house, so he had to go to the bathroom a few yards
outside his little shack. One night his mother heard
him screaming. His intestine had come out. We took
him to the hospital in a taxi. I'd never seen this.
What could be the matter? The diagnosis:
'Malnutrition, second degree.' What to do for him?
'Tell his mamá to give him an egg a day and a little
piece of meat. And milk, too.' Berta didn't even
have the money for the taxi we took to the hospital!
She had five more children, and her husband was a
garbage collector.*[7]

I have chosen the next account, despite its length, for the excellent
way in which it illustrates how the sort of generosity which does not
look at causes can harm the poor more than help them. It also
illustrates the extraordinary love and sharing among base community members, as they re-centre themselves on a truly biblically-
based faith.

Project Five-Two

*Unemployment is taking a hard toll among
metalworkers of Parque Santa Madalena, in São
Paulo. The crisis led the base communities to come
up with an imaginative solution: Project Five-Two.*

---

[7] Galdámez, pp. 21–2.

*Groups of five employed families adopt two
unemployed families and share with them basic food
items, such as beans, rice, and eggs. Currently over
100 families are involved.*

*'We received a gift from God and it must be
shared', says Sebastião de Andrade, who cannot get a
job because of a heart problem. Sebastião's wife and
young son are employed so they feel they can divide
what they have with others who are unemployed.*

*Adelaide de Oliveira, whose husband has been out
of a job for 9 months, pays $12 a month for a room
and kitchenette for the couple and four children,
one of them handicapped. 'The help we get is a lot
because it is essential; it is what we need to eat to
keep on living', says Adelaide. 'But', she is quick to
add, 'we haven't accommodated ourselves to this. It
is not a hand-out. My husband longs to find a job
so that we can be part of the Five who help, and no
longer the Two receiving help.'*

*Project Five-Two was inspired by the Biblical story
of the multiplication of the five loaves and two
fishes. Besides helping the families in need, it tries
to put pressure on society to pass work laws with
unemployment benefits and to create jobs for the
people. Charity alone does not resolve the problem.
Besides the immediate aim of helping people
survive, without causing passivity and dependency,
the project encourages the unemployed to unite in
seeking solutions and in demanding the right to
work. 'Food distribution is only one aspect of the
project, we also want to help families become aware
of the causes of unemployment', point out the
project participants, 'because the problem is one of
social structures which cannot be solved by
hand-outs'.*

*Project Five-Two riled the feelings of Hebe
Camargo, popular TV show hostess, who mobilized
her friends from society to donate a ton of beans and
rice, coffee and bread. Hebe went to Parque Santa
Madalena with a truck loaded with foodstuffs, as
well as a crew of videotape cameramen. She wanted
to film the food distribution to be used on her
Sunday night TV show, as a living example that it is*

always possible to share with others, no matter how little one has.

At Parque Santa Madalena, Hebe was received with a polite: 'Please excuse us, but we cannot accept your donations'.

Hebe was taken aback: 'What community is this where they don't allow people to help them? Whoever is hungry wants to eat, not to talk. I don't understand the spirit of this thing.'

Community members tried to explain. But Hebe wouldn't listen. Her plans were frustrated. On her next TV show she melted into tears as she lamented the refusal of her generous gift. For Hebe, charity was to take a few kilos of food to the needy, film the scene, then transmit it nationwide as an example for kind hearts to follow.

Not so for the base communities. The unemployed of Parque Santa Madalena did not feel inclined to appear on a TV show like beggars, with hands outstretched to receive bundles of food. 'We don't need assistance, but employment', they insisted, and went on to explain their reaction: 'May Dona Hebe forgive us if we are judging her wrongly, but it seems she came here to look for self-promotion when she should have respected our work . . . Five-Two is not a social aid fund but a work of consciousness raising . . . Dona Hebe could have helped, but without the TV cameras, for it is written that one should give with the right hand without the left hand knowing.'

Sebastião spoke for the community: 'We are not interested in publicity. We began this project reflecting on the Gospel, with love, and we don't want praise because we feel upset that our people should have to be suffering so much.'

Augusto Brito, youth leader, put it even stronger: 'Our plan is to become aware of the reasons for unemployment and at the same time show solidarity for our unemployed companions. No one here is giving alms. If we had accepted those donations we would have been prostituting Project Five-Two.'

Assistance might relieve the effects of unjust social organization but it does not touch the causes. A ton

*of food from the elite distributed to a handful of
families crushed at the bottom does not change the
structure of the pyramid. But when that handful at
the bottom prays, reflects, acts and moves together
for a common good, the pyramid begins to sway.*[8]

OPTION FOR THE POOR INCLUDES EVERYONE, BOTH RICH AND POOR

A common worry among first-world people is that basic Christian
communities are not for them, because 'the base' means 'the poor'
and they are not poor. But if this were so it would deny what we
have already seen about base communities being a way that is
universal, for all cultures. It is a way that goes back to the twelve
apostles and the early Church communities.

It is not so much that only 'base' people—poor people—can
belong, but rather that the communities have an option for the
base, an option for the poor.

Those communities that have come into existence so far in the
third world are certainly predominantly composed of the poor. But
in any definition there is always a qualifying phrase, 'mostly', or
'generally', or (as in this phrase from Leonardo Boff) 'primarily':
'they were given their name *comunidades eclesiales de base* because
they are communities primarily comprised of lower-class, grassroots
people, the base of society, as opposed to the pinnacle of power
in the social pyramid.'[9] We should remember that in the third
world, the great majority of people are poor. So it would be very
strange if the great majority of members of these communities,
which have an option for the poor, were not themselves poor people.

The base communities, then, are directed towards the base,
rather than confined to people at the base. And the communities
have this option for those at the base precisely because it is a constitutive part of the gospel message that the Church makes an
option for the poor.

So the base communities are not adding anything on to the basic
Christian message here. Rather, they are realizing and expressing

[8] Frances O'Gorman, *Base Communities in Brazil: Dynamics of a Journey,*
pp. 37–9. Sources: *Jornal do Brasil* (22 August 1983); *Folha de São Paulo*
(30 and 31 August 1983); *O Globo* (23 August, 1983).
[9] *Church, Charism and Power,* p. 125.

more powerfully and effectively a basic element of Christianity, that
the Good News is good news for everyone, but in a special way it
is good news for the poor.

It is not only rich people who have to come to terms with the
option for the poor. (I am using 'rich' simply as shorthand for 'those
who are not poor', which is rather cumbersome.) The poor too must
make an option for the poor, for simply happening to be poor does
not necessarily mean that you have made a commitment to the
cause of the poor. If you are poor and then win a lottery, do you
remain equally committed to the cause of the poor? Or do you lose
interest when your personal problem is solved?

So, if option for the poor is for rich and poor alike, can there
be middle-class base communities? Yes, there can. 'Class is not the
reference', says Carolee Chanona, 'faith is the reference.' But two
conditions should be fulfilled. Firstly, the Church should make it
a priority to support the development of base communities among
the poor rather than making communities of the rich and middle
classes their first concern. This is demanded by the option for the
poor which the Church as a whole takes, which refuses to see the
poor relegated to the end of the line in religious matters just as they
have been relegated to the end of the line in every other matter.
They may get the worst of education, housing and health care but
the Church chooses to give them the best of its own resources.

Secondly, a middle-class basic Christian community should itself
take an option for the poor. Being a base community means far
more than sorting out your own problems of liturgy and ministry
within the group. The internal benefits of the small Christian community are worthless unless there is also a missionary dimension,
as we saw on p. 61 above. And that means that the middle-class
members must go out, putting their gifts at the service of others
who may not live in their locality, and putting their gifts especially
at the service of the poor.

Along this line of thinking about the place of the well-off in a
basic Christian community, José Marins has said 'The rich are not
excluded. Nobody is excluded. But very often they exclude
themselves.' It is often said that liberation for the rich means con-
verting them from their attachment to riches.

It has certainly been found in practice that, even where attempts
have been made to form basic Christian communities among the
better off, they have not got off the ground in the way they have
done among the poor. But to find a few middle-class individuals
in the communities of the poor is not uncommon.

Actually joining the poor in their community, however, is not the only way in which a rich person can make an option for the poor. There are many different ways in which such an option may be expressed. At one extreme are those who want to experience what it is like to live in dire poverty, and who choose, probably for a limited period, to live like the poor. Nothing can compare with personal experience if we are to try to see the world through the eyes of the poor.

Then there are those who, while mixing on a regular basis with the poor, are aware that they have certain assets which the poor do not have — a telephone, perhaps, or a salary, or a typewriter, or a place on a committee that gives them some power. They may be aware that it is more use to the poor if they keep these assets, rather than give them up.

Michael Campbell-Johnston[10] has an example of this from his own experience. In El Salvador, living among the poor, he had no telephone, no telex, and no proper address (just a post office box). But agencies from the first world who wanted to send money for his work became impatient because they found it almost impossible to get in touch with him. Out of his option for the poor he was obliged to acquire some basics of modern technology.

At the other end of the scale are those who work with the rich, but who make use of their position to promote the cause of the poor. In this way it is possible, for example, to be a teacher in a fee-paying boarding school, and to increase awareness of the plight of the poor among people who will have influence in society. Of course it is also easy to con oneself that that is what one is doing, when one is simply taking a comfortable option for oneself. Some people who work in this way choose to divide their time between rich and poor, so they are constantly bridging the gaps of society and not losing touch with reality. Though there are dangers in choosing to promote option for the poor among the rich, the option can be a valid one. Very often it is a necessary first step in a gradual conversion to the option for the poor.

As the option for the poor is adopted in a more systematic way throughout the Church, and as base communities also become more widespread, it is to be expected that more middle-class basic Christian communities will develop.

---

[10] Until recently, provincial of the Jesuits for the British Province. He has now returned to Central America.

A little earlier we looked at part of a speech by Gustavo Gutiérrez at Worth Abbey. Here, in question time, he confesses that he personally is not poor, although as an Indian he comes from a very poor family. He illustrates the point that living in actual poverty is not the only way to make an option for the poor.

His speech is also important for hinting at the truth that there are other categories of marginalization besides material poverty alone. Gutiérrez speaks of 'the insignificant people'. Race and sex can also be reasons why people are treated as insignificant. It is sometimes said that a poor, black woman is triply marginalized.

I am not poor

Because of my family background I belonged to the poor in my country. Now that is not my case: I cannot say honestly I am the poor, because I am priest and because I have a situation in a big institution and because in my free time I am theologian. I cannot say I am insignificant. People from my family — they are still insignificant. It is not my case, though I try to be with the insignificant people.

I prefer to be clear, to be honest. I cannot play the game of saying you are rich persons living in England, I am poor coming from Peru. It is not true. I am not poor, because I am not insignificant. I have many problems in my life, sufferings as well, but I am not poor. I try to be committed to the poor — that is different. I try to be in the world of the poor — that is different. I try to share my life with them — but at the same time there is some difference in spite of my will. . . . I am personally not poor now. I was. It is not my case now.

And to be committed to the poor, the meaning is not to imitate the poor. I cannot imitate the poor. I speak very badly English, yes, but the poor people in my country they speak very badly Spanish. . . . I cannot imitate my people. I try to be with them — that is different.[11]

---

[11] A reflection given at Worth Abbey, 5 May 1989. Minor errors in English have been corrected. See also pp. 79–80 above.

The following two quotations from Leonardo Boff are along similar lines, as Boff explains that a middle-class or rich person can belong to a base community, but that they will be expected to share their expertise, for the benefit of the poor.

The place of the rich in a base community

The concerns taken up by these communities are universal, and they become universal in the measure in which the communities accept the universality of these concerns. Thus, these communities are not closed in on their own class interests; everyone, no matter of what class, who opts for justice and identifies with the struggles of the community will find a place there.[12]

A rich person can make an option for the poor by opting for justice, for social transformation, for political parties that present social alternatives. And by putting his or her expertise—as a doctor, lawyer, or engineer—at the service of organized communities.[13]

There is a true story told by José Marins about a base community in Chile, that speaks volumes. In joining the poor — in being at their side and showing ourselves their sisters and brothers—we should not diminish ourselves. There is no need to divest ourselves of any talent or skill that we possess. The aim is not to pretend to be other than what we are, but rather to put all that we have at the service of the poor.

The bricklayers and the lawyer

There was a basic Christian community among some people whose work was bricklaying. A lawyer used to come to this community, to join with the poor, and to learn from them what it meant to belong to a truly Christian community.

[12] Church, Charism and Power, p. 122.
[13] L. Boff in A New Way of Being Church: Interviews and Testimonies from Latin America Press, p. 7.

*Over the years he came to love the people more
and more. He began to identify with them to the
extent that he was troubled by his middle-class
status. 'I do not want there to go on being this
division between us', he thought to himself, 'that I
am a well-paid lawyer while they are poor
bricklayers. I must be brave enough to cross that
boundary and accept the same humble position.
Then I really will be able to say I am their brother.'*

*He went to the community and told them of his
decision. 'I am resolved', he explained, 'to give up
my job and my position, and to become truly one
with you. I will learn bricklaying from you, and so
become more fully a member of your community. I
believe that is what God is calling me to do.'*

*But as he spoke he saw some hesitation on their
faces. He had expected them to embrace him with
joy, but instead they held back and were whispering
among themselves. 'One moment', they said, 'We
need to have time to talk about this. Please wait
while we go away to discuss it.'*

*When they came back from their discussion their
faces were still grave. 'If this call has truly come to
you from God', they said, 'we will not stand in the
way. We must not oppose the will of God. But we
have a problem. We need a lawyer. Who will give
legal help to us poor people if you are no longer our
lawyer? We have talked together and reached a
decision. On the day that you leave the law to
become a bricklayer, we will choose one of our
number to study the law in your place.'*

The next story is not dissimilar, but it goes on to make a further
point. Those from the middle class who put their skills at the service
of the poor show a high degree of commitment: for they are not
acting for any class interest, but out of a truly Christian motivation.

Chico the surveyor

*To have a housing co-op we first had to clear the
land, level it, and stake it out in lots. So we needed
surveyors. A surveyor belonged to one of our*

communities, and he set to work. But there was too much to do. He started working overtime, but he told us he'd never finish even so. Then he asked for help from the university. The dean of the College of Agriculture put us in contact with a teacher, the teacher introduced us to Chico.

From that start, Chico showed himself to be the finest symbol of dedication and toil that we had ever known. He never took a day off, not even on weekends. He spent months measuring off and dividing up the lots. At night he would sketch out on paper what he'd done in the fields during the day. He would work right with our people, swinging a pickax or wielding a shovel. He was simply indefatigable. It was all volunteer work, and his generous, tireless unselfishness was astounding. He would let other jobs go to help us instead. Chico became a challenge to the whole community. He was a 'burning bush that was not burned up', a giver of self that didn't burn out. And from the midst of this bush, we heard the word of the Lord.

. . . Oh, now and then we'd wax indignant at the injustices suffered by our people or at some particular conflict or other. But generally we were pretty much wrapped up in ourselves and our own problems. Now here was this stranger, not even a member of our community, working for us tirelessly day and night. We understood what the sign of Chico meant and we were afraid—just as Moses was afraid when he discovered what his own rescue was going to mean in terms of a call. We understood that if we just stuck with our housing co-op, we'd be stuck with ourselves. We'd stay locked up in ourselves. Chico's dedication showed us a larger vocation. The liberation of a people. A whole people.[14]

[14] Faith of a People, p. 44.

OPTION FOR THE POOR MEANS THE POOR BECOME SUBJECTS

The great Brazilian educator, Paulo Freire, spoke out loudly about the false charity of rich people, when they appear to be philanthropic and generous but are actually ensuring that the same relation of domination continues. In that way the rich can go on feeling generous and the poor go on feeling grateful. His ideas are explained at greater length in Appendix 2.

One of the favourite texts of liberation theology is the Magnificat, which says just the opposite. Instead of saying that the mighty will go on being mighty, and the lowly go on being lowly—as though God had decreed this division of wealth and power—it says that the mighty would be put down from their thrones and the lowly would be exalted.

An underlying assumption of the base communities is that there is a fundamental equality of rich and poor, of powerful and powerless, in which roles can readily be reversed. And so true generosity means empowering people, enabling relationships to change so that the lowly can do things they never imagined would be possible, and so that the mighty divest themselves of the control they have been used to exercising. Then those who have played a passive role, suffering poverty and possibly receiving others' generosity, move to playing an active role, becoming agents of change, and subjects of history.

It is not just a matter of letting the poor have an equal share of the action, but of recognizing that they have a privileged role in transforming the world. Their ears are open to hear the good news and their hearts are not weighed down by the distractions of earthly treasures. 'In impoverishment, we discover the central reference of life', says José Marins. From that vision of what lies at the heart of life, we can start basic Christian community. This is, after all, what happened in the beginning, when fishermen became apostles.

For this to happen, it is essential that the rich change their mentality, from the paternalistic 'doing things for the poor', to the respectful 'doing things *with* the poor'. The message was well summed up in a little mime I saw done by a group from Dutch base communities: a man stood on a chair, and tried to pull a woman up from the ground. She would get so far up, but then be unable to stand and fall back to the floor again. After several attempts to raise her, the man changed his tactic. He stepped down from his chair and went down to her level. This time the two rose together, slowly, each one helping the other, the man helping the woman, and the woman helping the man. At last they both stood up straight side by side.

This poem is written by an Aboriginal Australian woman:

Growth not decay

If you have come
to help me
you are wasting
your time.

But

If you have come
because
your liberation
is bound up
with mine
then let us work
together.

Next we have a theological statement from Leonardo Boff, which brings together some key concepts in the way option for the poor is understood, and in particular the dignity of the poor who become historical subjects. The type of Church Boff is speaking of is the basic ecclesial communities.

The privileged status of the poor

This type of Church presupposes what was
crystallized at the Latin American bishops' meeting
at Puebla in 1979: a preferential option for the poor.
The exact meaning of this option is to recognize the
privileged status of the poor as the new and
emerging historical subject which will carry on the
Christian project in the world. The poor, here, are
not understood simply as those in need; they are in
need but they are also the group with a historical
strength, a capacity for change, and a potential for
evangelization. The Church reaches out to them

*directly, not through the state or the ruling classes.
Thus, we are no longer speaking of a Church for the
poor but rather a Church of and with the poor.
From this option for and insertion among the poor
the Church begins to define its relationship with all
other social classes. It does not lose its catholicity; its
catholicity becomes real and not merely a matter of
rhetoric. The Church is directed toward all, but begins
from the poor, from their desires and struggles.*[15]

One of the most compelling presentations of option for the poor
that I know is this statement by the Jesuit Refugee Service about
how they see their work with refugees.

Seeing the world through the eyes of the poor

*We want to place special emphasis on being with
rather than doing for. We want our presence among
refugees to be one of sharing with them, of
accompaniment, of walking together along the same
path. In so far as possible, we want to feel what they
have felt, suffer as they have, share the same hopes
and aspirations, see the world through their eyes.
We ourselves would like to become one with the
poor and oppressed peoples so that, all together, we
can begin the search for a new life.*

*This attempt to identify with the poor and
rejected, however hesitant and imperfect, has
brought us untold blessings. For by their very
poverty they teach us to become detached from
material possessions and our own selves. Their
insecurity and uncertainty about the future show us
how not to rely merely on ourselves or on human
planning. Their cultural values and simple dignity as
human beings remind us that a person's worth is
determined by what he is rather than by what he
has. Their openness and generosity so often challenge
us to share with them and others all that we have*

[15] Church, Charism and Power, pp. 9–10. For the meaning of **subject**,
project and **insertion** see Appendix 1.

*and are. Their happiness and laughter in the midst
of adversity help us to understand the true meaning
of suffering. Their deep faith and unfailing hope
lead us to rediscover these spiritual values in our own
lives. In a word, we have found Christ again in the
faces and lives of these abandoned people, a Christ
who is beckoning and calling us to follow Him.*[16]

OPTION FOR THE POOR MEANS ORGANIZATION

People from base communities often talk of the need to organize. For example, there is a slogan used by the Movement of Female Rural Workers[17] in Brazil: 'Women who struggle and are organized bring to birth the new society'.[18]

It can take a while to realize the full weight of what the base communities mean by organization. For us in the first world, organization can almost smack of bureaucracy. But in the third world, it is not that at all, and we need to go back to first principles.

Alone, we are vulnerable and powerless. Strength lies in numbers. A people is organized when they have worked out how to convert a disorganized crowd into a coherent, coordinated body that can achieve goals. There must be order, not chaos; there must be communication, not ignorance; there must be accepted leaders, not manipulation by a few pushy entrepreneurs; and so on. Any community needs some organization, and the bigger the network of communities, the better the organization needs to be.

When people from the base communities talk of becoming organized, they do not mean at all that someone should come in from outside to organize them, and that they will do what they are told because otherwise they are afraid of chaos. It is not that at all.

---

[16] Statement by the Jesuit Refugee Service, Seven Fountains, Chiang Mai, Thailand, 21 November 1985.

[17] *Movimento de Mulheres Trabalhadoras Rurais.*

[18] *Mulher que luta organizada gera a nova sociedade.* I have this on a T-shirt with a strikingly feminist picture to go with it. A woman, wearing a pretty dress, straw hat and earrings, with a shopping basket and a baby in one arm, and a hoe in the other, is striding, barefoot and determined, over a hill-top. Behind her shoulder follows a man, carrying another agricultural tool. In the sky around float various banners, one of which reads 'CEBs'.

When they talk of becoming organized, they mean that the people should organize themselves. Only then will the organization hold firm under pressure and command the allegiance of all the members.

Of course waiting while a people organize themselves can take a lot longer than sending someone in to take control. But that is just part of the message we have to learn from basic Christian community — that it is a process, and it takes time. But the end product is far better grounded than an externally imposed structure.

The following exercise that I took part in while on a Marins' workshop taught me more about how a people should organize than anything I could have learned from reading books. At the same time it was a window onto the whole of political life. If we really learnt the lessons of this exercise, then could we not transform the world?

The Knot

Carolee Chanona took the whole workshop, nearly seventy people, out onto the lawn. We had already formed ourselves into ten groups, each with its own self-chosen name. So there we all were on the grass on a lazy summer's afternoon — Expectancy and Thrishna (thirst), Simplicity and the Apologists, the Beyondists and Blurred Vision, the Cucumber Group, the Listening Group, Struggling Through and Que Sera.

Carolee asked for eleven volunteers. She asked them to stand in a circle and cross their right arm over their left, then to join hands with the next-but-one. Next she told them to rearrange themselves so they were all facing outwards and no one had their arms crossed. They must not let go of the hand they were holding, though they could adjust their grip so they were not twisting anyone's wrist. The volunteer group did the exercise easily.

Now she asked the entire group of nearly seventy to do the same. This was more tricky. Knots kept on forming. Each time we tried to untangle the knot, a new knot would form somewhere else. We must have spent a good ten minutes, weaving our human chain in and out, over and under, trying to untie the knot.

Those who were in a free stretch looked triumphant and carefree, looking scathingly over their shoulders at those in the knot, as though they were the cause, not the victims, of the problem. A minute later the knot had moved along and those who had been free were now the ones bent over and contorted.

Some became convinced that we would never solve the problem. 'It just goes to show you cannot do a thing like this in a big group' they said. Soon we all lost interest in our goal and just enjoyed the clambering.

All the while this was going on, a woman with a bad leg who could not join in was sitting on the ground nearby. At first she tried to make a verbal contribution, but people generally did not hear. They were too involved in their own task. After a while she gave up trying and lost interest in the process.

Then Carolee clapped her hands and told us to go back to our original groups, and to try to sort it out from there. Ten little groups formed around the lawn. We tried out the exercise in miniature, and after a few minutes discovered how to do it. If you watched carefully in a small group, it was easy to pick out the secret of success.

How could we communicate the truth we had discovered to the other seventy? They were rather a large number to talk to all at once in the open air. You would have to shout, and even so there would be little groups talking among themselves who would not be listening. So there was a communication problem.

What is more, it was not just our group who had unlocked the secret. Around the lawn were several groups who had found the key, and were eager to communicate it to the rest. We would shout each other down, and we might have quite different ways of explaining it. Each group wanted to be the one to tell the others how to do it. So there was an authority problem as well.

Our group thought of the idea of going round each group asking a delegate to come to a central meeting. But even as we were beginning to go to the first group, there were others gathering in the centre with the same idea, calling for delegates at a conference. My group sent me.

One person was saying, 'My group has given me authority to come here for discussion and sharing of ideas. But they have made it plain that I have no power to make decisions on their behalf. I have to return to my group with any suggestion before it can be agreed.'

Meanwhile a couple of others were jumping up and down impatiently. 'Look it's easy', they were saying. 'We have worked it out. All you do is this . . .'

At the same time people from around the lawn who were not delegates were trying to join in on the conversation. The delegates, who had now formed a group of their own, were annoyed by this, as it slowed down the conference. It took quite long enough to let ten delegates all have an equal say, without admitting voices from the background.

As the conference of delegates split up to return to base, to share their new knowledge of how to untie the knot, two or three of the last to leave made a decision between themselves. 'We are going to need a leader', a man said to a girl. 'When we try again, you had better be the one to call out instructions.'

The seventy joined hands in the big circle once more, and the girl took charge. Some of us delegates were surprised as we had not remembered this arrangement: it had been made after we had left the meeting. But despite some slight resentment the method worked beautifully. With one person calling out step by step we achieved our task almost at once, and soon were standing—with a whoop of joy—all facing outwards, with no knots.

After the praxis came the evaluation, first in small groups and then all together. The question was 'What have we learned?'

We had learned that a structural fault in society is

everyone's problem. Unless the problem is properly understood, analysed and solved you merely move it along, so that someone else will suffer tomorrow. You cannot really have liberation for some without liberation for all.

We had learned that to mobilize the people you need careful planning. Otherwise much time is lost. Any deficiencies at the local level become much graver when they are multiplied at a larger level. It is easier to carry passengers in a small group than in a big one.

We had learned that a large number cannot work together unless there is some form of delegation or accepted leadership. A refusal to organize in this way — giving responsibility to some people — means that large group tasks will never be achieved. Then you will never get beyond a haphazard collection of small communities that achieve far less than they are capable of.

We had learned that the right leader for a specific task is not necessarily the right person for other duties. Delegation was for the sake of achieving an end, not a higher status.

We had learned that we must stop and pay attention to the sick and disabled if they are not to be excluded totally from the process.

We had learned that unless we have faith that the goal is possible, and the interest to work for it, then we will never achieve it. It is easy to become diverted into making the process the goal, so we have no impetus to move on to the next stage.

We had learned that people resent being told what to do. They like to discover for themselves, and to make the process their own. And at the same time they like to impose their own model on others, as though they were the only ones with privileged experience. We may share a common goal but have different techniques for getting there, that are equally valid.

We had learned that we must not expect others to come to us, but we must be prepared to go to them. And that the best place for conferring is neutral ground where everyone feels equal.

> *We had learned that those who are quick to see*
> *what is needed must be patient, while the slower*
> *ones learn. Only when everyone has understood—*
> *maybe not every detail but the essential points—can*
> *the people move forward together.*
> *Finally we had learned that to achieve a large*
> *group task together is very satisfying, and binds the*
> *big community together.*

When I read Leonardo Boff's *Ecclesiogenesis*—which was a seminal book for me—I was struck by the claim that 'When the people organize, they show what society ought to be: strong and invincible'.[19] It sounds great, but does it actually happen?

Often it does not, because the people's organization falls down for one reason or another. Those who had felt great solidarity before they were confronted by any opposition, often find that once the challenge comes, the ranks break open and former resolves are questioned. As Jesus pointed out, if you are planning to go to war you have to sit down and work out in advance if your forces will be able to withstand the forces of the enemy (Luke 14:31).

But in a way even such failures prove the point. If action fails because of lack of solidarity and organization among the people under pressure, then solidarity and organization are the crucial factors for success.

The next, long passage from Niall O'Brien's powerful account of building basic Christian communities in the Philippines, illustrates with humour and realism the difficulties and strengths of an organized action by the people. Ultimately the people, acting in a wholly peaceful fashion, are able to disarm and defeat the men of violence. We even see the beginning of a change of heart in the bandit.

Overpowering Little Angel

> *'Little Angel' lived in Amian, one of the hard-to-get-*
> *at parts of our parish. He had been involved in two*
> *known slayings and was credited with many more.*
> *He was said to eat the ears of the victims. Twenty-*
> *seven was the number cited, and I had that from*
> *one of my own Christian community leaders who*

[19] p. 44.

*had been forced to sit down and watch him eat the
ears. There were two or three weak Christian
communities in the area. They were in a state of
shock and panic. Most of the people in that area
were now no longer sleeping in their houses at
night.*

*But what was the answer? Some were saying:
'Leave it to the boys.' This when translated meant
that the N.P.A. [New People's Army] would send
someone in to investigate and deliver judgment. The
investigators would be young people not without
heart and compassion but the trial would take place
under the stress of 'war'. They had no prison and if
the person was found guilty the punishment, when
warnings had failed, could hardly be less than death.*

*I had an even more basic difficulty with the very
idea of calling in outsiders to solve the problem.
Could not the people come up with something
themselves? Once they called in outsiders they
became that much more dependent, and we were
back to the old need to have someone to look up to
and defend us. When some Robin Hood 'knocked
off' the offender the people could go back to their
houses but no one had changed, no one had grown.
The tumour had been excised but no antibodies had
been developed in the system to stop its recurrence.
We would have to do something ourselves.*

*Our parish council called on Brian for advice
because we knew that his communities had been
doing just this and, in fact, they had cleared up a
much graver situation in their own areas without
outside help.*

*Brian's communities had developed various
methods of nonviolent self-defense. One of the basic
principles in Brian's approach was: 'We have the
numbers; we are like ants. If a few of them come
around the place, they are easily brushed away or
killed. If a whole nest of them swarms around you,
you move away.'*

*We all agreed that the Christian community
approach is essentially preventive. Strong
communities with a good system of communication
between them also were the best deterrents to*

marauders. The problem with Amian was that there were no strong communities, and I noticed myself that those other areas of the parish where the communities were weak were also the areas which had the most problems with night banditry.

First Brian's core group met with our core group. Then they came back and met with the full parish council — the presidents and officers of the mini-parishes (this came to about thirty-five people). The discussion went on far into the night and they finally came up with a plan. We would hold a Mass at the house of Little Angel. Though it was way in the back of beyond a thousand people would converge on the place, and while we were there we would ask Little Angel to lay down his arms. Brian's group had done this many times, so they had all the details of how people should travel, what they should do if other groups tried to stop them, what to do if the army appeared, how to avoid panic, how to keep a check on participants to stop infiltration by troublemakers, what if it rained and the rivers rose, and so on.

The final meeting took place without Brian's group. Our core group chaired the meeting and all the details were drawn up. Each mini-parish had to guarantee a certain number of members from each community and they had to be reliable people.

Back in my room I could feel the anxiety in the air. There was one thing I had not said, because I felt they were not ready for it, and that was that I believed that Little Angel was just like the rest of us: not an evil man, but just someone who knew no better and whom no one had ever helped along the way.

I prayed and lay down to wait for dawn when we would start out. Tonight, I said to myself, many people in the communities are lying awake wondering if they should go or not. Some wives are dissuading husbands and some husbands are dissuading wives. They are reviewing their decision and fighting their fear. But as they overcome their fears they themselves are growing; I can almost feel the people growing!

But I was worried too because if this failed—our first major group attempt at active nonviolence—then people would say there was only one way and that was the gun.

In the morning we set off at a trot. At various points along the way we were joined by groups from the different communities. As we neared the house the tension grew. For a long time now people had avoided even the vicinity of this house like an evil place.

Little Angel was outside his house. He had a large blade in his hand. He was puzzled over the arrival of so many people. I walked up to him. I was trembling. I explained to him that we were coming to say Mass. He surprised me by saying: 'Someone said you might come to say Mass so I was about to kill a rooster for you.' I said: 'Why not come upstairs and have a chat with me first?' We went up together. I tried to conceal my nervousness as I asked him to lay aside the knife, which I then passed out the window. By this time a huge crowd had gathered outside the house. I then explained to him why we had come.

The tension in the crowd was something terrible. At one stage some people were standing on a bench which broke with a crack like the sound of gunshot: people scattered in all directions in a panic. A couple of the toughest appeared at the door with a 'let us at him' look on their faces. I said that they could not touch him because he had agreed to hand over all his weapons. They made a rush at him, but I kept between him and them. It was a charade. It had not been in the original plan, and I felt ashamed of it afterward, but from this distance it is hard to understand the strain and suspense we were all under.

When I had pushed them back he went to an inner room and brought out his knives and amulets and membership forms for what he called the 'N.P.A.–Salvatore'. And handed them over.

Then we asked him to go to the window and ask his followers to do likewise, because many of his group, when they saw all the people converging on

Little Angel's house, had tagged along to see what was going to happen. The crowd gained in courage and began to point out those who belonged to Little Angel's gang, and collected their weapons and amulets. All in all it amounted to a complete sackful. Then all his followers were rounded up and put in one place and we addressed the crowd as to what should be done.

Now their anger came out as they remembered the killings and how he had terrorized them for so long, and one or two voices began to demand that Little Angel be killed. I explained that that was against our principles and we would become like those we were condemning.

Eventually some in the crowd said he should be exiled from the place. That in fact had been the decision reached by the communities in their own preliminary discussions, so I asked Little Angel if he had any place to go and he said his grandmother had a place in a faraway part of the mountains. It was agreed that he should leave immediately. The rest of the gang were told they could not be members of the Christian community until they had proved themselves.

Then began the Mass of thanksgiving. I explained why I was refusing Communion to Little Angel and his followers and I tried to develop the meaning of being a community from this example.

Little Angel came home with us, and during the night Junior and Baby spent time pointing out gently but firmly why what he had been doing was wrong. I also spent some time with him. The most interesting thing that emerged from my long conversation with Little Angel was the proof for me that the army were in fact behind this so-called N.P.A.–Salvatore group. It was a way of discrediting the N.P.A. and gave the army justification for sweeping into our areas which did not have any real N.P.A. presence. Was that why every attempt to have Little Angel arrested had come to nothing?

On the wall in the room where Little Angel slept that night we had a huge picture eight feet long by four feet wide, of Christ being scourged. In medieval

*style the artist, Lino Montebon, had introduced
around the central scourging picture vignettes
illustrating life in Negros, such as land-grabbing,
army atrocities, property speculation, usury, unfair
wages, religious hypocrisy, robbery, and rape: there
was something for everyone. The following morning
Little Angel spoke spontaneously for the first time.
Up to this point he had just been answering
questions. He led me over to the picture of the
scourging and, pointing at one of the Roman soldiers
who held a cat-o'-nine-tails, said: 'That's me'.*

*The crowd of ordinary men and women coming all
the way to that lonely part of the mountain to
protest, the ritual excommunication, fear, the little
talks in the night, had made Little Angel think. The
simple picture filled with symbols he understood
spoke to him, and he used it to speak to us.*[20]

OPTION FOR THE POOR MEANS RESPONSIBILITY FOR THE LOCALITY

We saw earlier[21] how much base communities are associated with
the locality, from the point of view of the base community being
the basic cell of the Church. Now we look at the local basis from
another angle — that of option for the poor.

The poor, because they are poor, have no voice[22] and are
usually forgotten. All over the world are millions and millions of
poor, and how are we to know what their needs are or even if they
exist? Even within a country like Britain, which has millions of
unemployed people, it is easy for them to drop out of the headlines
of the news and rarely appear on even a feature page. We are so
busy reporting on all the goings-on of people with jobs and power
and influence that we simply do not notice what is happening to
the others, who are not raising their voices but rather suffering
humiliation. So often the poor slip further and further from
sight — not because of malice, but simply because of ignorance.

[20] *Revolution from the Heart*, pp. 209–18. This version is much
abbreviated for reasons of space, and it is well worth reading the full
chapter 39 from the original book.
[21] On pp. 16–18.
[22] Archbishop Romero was often called 'The voice of the voiceless'.

How can we notice the silent masses, if we have not a geographical network, covering every area, attuned to needs in every hidden corner of the country, and of the world? The parish system, which covers the ground systematically, is an enormous resource for simply discovering the truth about poverty.

The base community system, if it operates geographically, can be a far more effective resource: for instead of a single priest trying to keep up to date on the needs of several thousand people, there is a community in every little group of streets. And so it is a resource for responding to local needs that are unmet—lonely old people confined to the house, the families of the imprisoned, the anguished husband of a wife dying of cancer . . . And at the same time it can become a channel of information to the outside world.

José Marins tells a story that highlights the need for Christians to take on a minimum of local responsibility. In the Second World War there was a Benedictine monastery, quite close to one of the concentration camps. At the end of the war, when the truth came out, someone asked one of the monks what he had done, or said, or even thought, about that concentration camp. He replied that he had not known what happened there. He was very busy, you see, working hard for the Church in all sorts of ways—apostolic work, worthwhile work, work for God . . . One cannot do everything. How could he be blamed for not knowing what was happening in the local concentration camp?

More recently in Argentina, Marins continues, there was a torture chamber. Thirty thousand people disappeared in Argentina during the decade of repression, many of them in just such places as that torture chamber. When the truth came out about that, the parish priest was asked how he had coped with living so close to such a place. He replied he had not known it existed. He too was very busy, doing so many good works. He did not have time to notice the torture chamber.

Somehow we know that these answers will not do. And yet it could be us, answering, excusing ourselves for not knowing what is happening next door to us. As one African sister said on a visit to the first world: if you want to be in solidarity with us, find the poverty in your own back yard.

When Niall O'Brien was trying to get across the message of basic Christian communities to his far-flung parishioners in the island of Negros, in the Philippines, he told them this story.

If Na-Salayan had had a Christian community

'So you want to start a Christian community. Well it's like this . . .' And I would tell them the following story: 'The man who cut the grass for this thatch'—pointing to the roof of the convento —*lives out in Na-Salayan. A few weeks ago he walked in all the way from that place, which is about ten kilometers away, carrying his wife on his back. As he walked his little child of three ran along beside him clinging to his trouser leg. And another child of eight carried the baby. His wife was so far gone with T.B. that she was only bones. He told me that for a year she has not been able to sleep well. They have no pillow, so at night when they lay down he would stretch out his arm and she would lie on it the whole night. if Na-Salayan had had a Christian community, that man would not have walked in alone. The men of the hamlet would have carried his wife in a baby's hammock, the women would have looked after the children, and the community health committee would have looked for medicines for the sick woman and told us about her condition months ago. Now it is certainly too late. You have a Christian community when you can lie down at night knowing that in your village no one is sick who is not being attended to, no one is persecuted who is not being helped, no one is lonely who is not being visited.*[23]

OPTION FOR THE POOR AFFIRMS CULTURE AND HISTORY

We saw right back at the beginning of Chapter 1 that basic ecclesial communities are for all cultures. Now is the time to explore that connection with culture more fully.

This is one of the big differences between basic communities and the centralized movements, which follow a set pattern or programme wherever they occur—using the same books or posters, or

[23] *Revolution from the Heart*, pp. 128–9.

following the same structure for the meeting. Base communities are far more varied. There is no pattern, no programme, no uniformity. They take their form from the local base, so they grow upwards ✗ like a tree, rather than spreading downwards like the rays of the sun.

And so, points out Carolee Chanona, 'There will never be two basic Christian communities alike. This does not mean a split in the Church. But different realities will give basic Christian community a new face. If they were the same we would be being unfaithful.'

Closely allied to culture is the history of the people. Carolee explains, 'Without a history, a people has no identity. Without an identity, a people cannot forge a future.' So an important part of building a community is to recall where we come from, so that we are able to know who we are, and to look to where we are going.

When I attended the regular Monday evening meeting of base community coordinators in Managua, Nicaragua, I witnessed an example of this. Each team of coordinators (there were two from each community) was invited to recall the history of their community, including telling us which song or songs had helped them on their journey. Soon the hall was full of people picking up snatches of song, as they re-affirmed each community's own path of salvation history.

The poor may have a very poor self-image, being marginalized in society, and so it may take a while before they begin to feel proud of their culture and history. Bishop Jorge Marskell, from the Itacoatiara region of Brazil, told me it was only recently that his people had felt able to recognize their Indian ancestry, and admit to having Indian blood in them. But now it was becoming a point of pride.

Again and again we find people falling prey to the lure of what has sometimes been called Coca-Cola-ization[24] – the cultural imperialism of the USA, which leads to people all around the world wanting to drink Coca-Cola, to wear blue jeans and to eat hamburgers.

One of the tasks of base community is to be an influence in the ✗ opposite direction, away from the materialism of imitating the richest culture in the world, towards a sense of pride in being one of God's beloved people, for 'blessed are the poor'.

The particular contribution of the Bishops' Conference at Santo

---

[24] The Sri Lankan theologian Aloysius Pieris has used this term.

Domingo[25] in 1992 is said to be its affirmation of the value of culture.

This extract shows how an affirmation of local culture was given a high priority right back at the beginnings of basic Christian communities in Bolivia. This report was published in 1974, but refers back to considerably earlier.

Catechists among the Aymara

Among the basic community experiments in Bolivia those of the Altiplano of La Paz stand out. The idea originated in 1956 when the foreign priests noticed the lack of communication between themselves and the Aymara communities.

The priests in charge of these communities had to be accompanied by a group of more educated peasants who functioned as translators and collaborators. After some time they felt that these men should be given some special ad hoc *training. The Maryknoll Fathers opened the first training centre at Peñas.*

At the beginning these catechists merely repeated the lessons given by the priest. Gradually they created a kind of identity of their own. At present [1974] there are about 900 catechists on the Altiplano, and if we add those that work on the Peruvian border there are 2,000. However, if we count only the full-time members this figure must be reduced to more humble proportions.

Care is taken that these people are not cut off from their milieu and surroundings during their training. The community itself selects those it thinks most suitable for this service. For the first week they follow a catechetical course in the parish which prepares them for their first tasks. After a few months they are sent to the centre in Peñas or Chulumani where they follow a three-week course. Yet, according to an enquiry set up in 15 parishes of the Altiplano, they prefer to be trained on the spot

[25] For **Santo Domingo** see Appendix 1.

so that they will be better adapted to their milieu . . .

The leaders' task is not limited to religion but embraces the whole of human advancement in culture, economics, health and the promotion of woman in society. Care is therefore taken to train different people for different functions in the community in order that each can find his own way and the community can avoid becoming dependent on 'the local bosses'. Education for literacy is well organized in collaboration with the Ministry of Education and Radio 'San Cristobal' and with the help of teachers and educational leaders under the supervision of the parish team.

Moreover, a start is also made with the building up of Aymara culture, an effort very popular with the young people who felt inferior to the city population and now are discovering the values specific to their own culture. For this reason efforts are made in order that each community may have a 'house of culture' with a library.

Two priests travel up and down the region to train the peasants in trade unionism, politics and economics. Every three months they organize courses for the leaders, teaching them the history of their country, their rights, and the technics of community leadership.

All this work is aimed at creating an indigenous Church with its own culture, its liturgy, its religious leaders and its social workers.[26]

Although the need to affirm the authentic culture of the people is most urgent among the poor, it applies to everyone. It would be a mistake for those from rich and privileged backgrounds to find nothing among their own people of which they could be proud.

Along these lines I recall one of Marins' workshops, with a very international gathering, where we split into groups according to our origins and produced a symbol for our people. The African group brought a candle stuck into rich, black earth, surrounded by barbed wire. Those from the Americas brought a painting of a cross made

[26] This comes from the same source as the extract on p. 55.

from a palm tree. The Asian peoples brought a mask, which could be happy, or sad.

As for the British, those from the bleak, industrial North of England brought a chipped brick. The fiery Celts brought fire as their symbol. Those from the Midlands brought a UB40 card — the card of the unemployed. While those from the then economically thriving south — among which I found myself — brought a black briefcase, a credit card, a Filofax, and a red rose: we felt quite pleased with our slightly ironic acknowledgement of the symbols of our over-privileged people.

The next passage shows the South African Black Consciousness leader, Steve Biko, prodding even those from the culture of the oppressor into being proud of their origins. Biko is out driving his car when he sees some hitchhikers.

The hitchhikers

On the way through the arid, flat Orange Free State he grew bored and lonely and gave a lift to two young whites. They had seemed reluctant to talk, and as company and conversation had been his aim in giving them a lift (they were hitchhiking all the way to Johannesburg) he decided to draw them out.

'Are you boys English-speaking or Afrikaans-speaking?' he asked.

After some hesitation one of them said: 'We're both English-speaking.' But Steve could detect from their accent that they were Afrikaners.

'What a pity,' he said, 'I was hoping you were Afrikaans-speaking because I want to improve my Afrikaans and I hoped to get some practice.'

No response.

'Kom, praat met my [Come speak with me]', he said in Afrikaans.

'No, we don't know Afrikaans much', one of them replied. But the more English he spoke the more they struggled, until eventually he challenged them with a smile: 'Come on, you're Afrikaans-speaking, aren't you?' With great reluctance they admitted it.

'Why did you deny it?' he persisted. Well, they said, they knew that black people didn't like Afrikaners. Typically, Steve then delivered a long lecture to the effect that people should never, under

any circumstances, be ashamed or reticent about their origins or race or culture. 'There's nothing to be ashamed of in language or culture. In fact you should be proud of these things!' After that they became relaxed and friendly and chatted all the way to Johannesburg. In Afrikaans![27]

The urgent need for inculturation[28] in the Church, to build up the local people's pride in their origins, is illustrated by the following horrifying example from the Amazon region of Brazil:

Religion had to come from abroad

Recently a bishop confided in us that in an area of his Prelature, the Catholic people received the new parish priest with much mistrust. It was the first time a native priest of the same size, colour and speech as the village people had appeared in the church to celebrate mass. The people felt disorientated. They received him with mistrust and sent to ask the bishop if that man could really be a Catholic priest. All the ministers of God that they had known in their life were foreigners — very different from the local people. Religion was something which had to come from abroad, like electrical equipment and every other good product.[29]

Another passage from the same book points up the dangers of a style of evangelizing that takes no account of inculturation. We are in the Philippines.

Enrolling members for the 'American way of life'

From the window of my room, on the second floor, my gaze followed two young men who some way off were coming along the dirt road. They were no more

[27] Donald Woods, *Biko* (Penguin, 1979), pp. 76–7.
[28] See Appendix 1.
[29] José Marins, *¿Salir o Quedarse?*, p. 126.

than twenty years of age. When I saw them pass the side of the house where we are, their white faces, blue eyes, western nose and manner of dressing, marked them as out of tune with our cultural surroundings. Blue trousers (but not jeans), white shirt (but cut in a military style), a tie, and a 'robot' style which has their message well recorded for them to recite. Blond, very Saxon. They carry books, magazines, some simple, direct phrases to answer fifteen questions which people are accustomed to make. They have the unchanging task of visiting house by house, offering their literature and their religion, along with their ideology and their culture . . . conscientiously dedicated, with admirable insistence, to their mission of destroying the Catholic faith and of enrolling new members for their sect and for the 'American way of life'. In Buenos Aires as in La Paz, in Quezon City as in Bogotá, in Tokyo as in Mexico City, they are going to be organizing their 'church', and in many places they are equally leaving behind their majestic temples, perfect in style (perhaps) for North America . . . but totally alien from the local cultures and suitably set apart from their reality.[30]

In Buenos Aires as in La Paz, and, it seems, in Guatemala as in the Philippines, to judge from this uncannily similar description by Jonathan Evan Maslow, who went to Guatemala as a bird-watcher.

The Apparition

It was just then that the Apparition appeared. He was as young, blond, clean-shaven, close-cropped, sanitized and square a gringo as you'd come across at your front door in the States on Sunday morning, pushing his version of piety. He was dressed in an absurdly clean white, short-sleeved business shirt, pressed blue slacks, and a thin black knit tie. . . . The Apparition said he was a missionary for a Protestant evangelical sect and had been in the

[30] *¿Salir o Quedarse?*, pp. 125–6.

highlands a few months trying to convert the
locals . . .
 'You just can't believe all the things you hear.
Why, if there weren't freedom of religion down
here, our mission wouldn't be able to come here and
hold meetings in the first place.'
 'We've been noticing how many of the churches
are closed. Seems like some priests have disappeared.'
 'Who told you that? I haven't heard anything
about that . . . I've been all over. Some time here,
some time there. Wherever Jesus needs me, that's
where I go!'
 'And where did Jesus need you before Guatemala?'
 The Apparition tensed, and said, 'Fort Bragg,
North Carolina.'
 . . . 'Look, let's stop kidding each other', I said.
'We both know that's where military intelligence
operations are headquartered.'
 'Gee, I wouldn't know anything about that.'[31]

The final passage illustrates a very different approach to evangelization—one that embraces inculturation, dialogue and option for the poor, as well as proclamation of the gospel.

In the São Miguel region of São Paulo, the local bishop, Dom Angélico Bernardino Sândalo,[32] promoted Popular Radio stations, providing resources and personnel to help the local communities. Popular Radio is a very simple device—a group of loudspeakers, stuck usually on the roof of the church, which blares out local notices as they are needed and perhaps a specially made programme for a couple of hours a week.

Many local communities want to play music from the USA. They are not prevented, for that would be dictatorial and so against base community principle, but Brazilian music is more positively encouraged. Dom Angélico's team for. Popular Radio announced as their objectives:

---

[31] *Bird of Life, Bird of Death*, pp. 150–2.
[32] Until the Vatican reorganized the diocese of São Paulo (Cardinal Arns' diocese) in 1989.

Objectives of Popular Radio

—To recover the voice of the people, their religiosity, their culture, their history, their traditions, their legends and myths . . .

— To evangelize—proposing action that can transform society. To promote common tasks.

—To broadcast the life of the community. To support the organization and struggles of the community.

—To give basic information. To communicate the problems and the hopes of the people.

—To defend the people's artists, poetry, music, festivals. To create participation at every level. To form and train new leaders.

As we continued along these lines we began to notice that the radio was no longer a dream but was becoming part of the history of our people. The way is hard but we persist because we believe in the power of the people's word.[33]

[33] Rádio do Povo, p. 21.

4

Base community is about the base of the Church — the laity

We come now to the fourth sense of basic — the fourth mark of the base community. It is more often recognized that 'base' refers to the base of society, than that it also refers to the base of the Church — to the people at the bottom, without status, authority or power in ecclesial affairs, that is, the laity.

Yet the liberation theologians stress the base community's basis among the laity, alongside its basis among the poor. 'The members of these communities are generally poor and from the base of society (the lower classes) and from the base of the Church (the laity).'[1]

Of course, as we saw with the poor, that does not mean you cannot belong to a base community unless you are a layperson. In fact, without the participation or approval of priests and sisters, and the pastoral strategy of favourable bishops, base communities would barely have got off the ground. But it does mean there is a strong lay thrust and a discovery of the potential of the laity. It is what we might call an option for the laity: 'Although the great majority of basic church communities owe their origin to a priest or a member of a religious order, they nevertheless basically constitute

[1] Leonardo Boff, *Church, Charism and Power*, p. 125.

a lay movement. The laity carry forward the cause of the gospel here.'[2]

THERE IS A MULTIPLICITY OF MINISTRIES IN BASE COMMUNITY

We have seen how the poor and the humble are enabled to find a voice and to explore their potential, within the supportive embrace of a Christian community that knows and loves them. But what is true about the liberation of the poor, is obviously equally true about the liberation of the laity.

It is not just a matter of lay people looking for something to do in order to feel useful: every community has all sorts of needs that must be fulfilled, so there is no lack of urgent work to be done. The distinctive insight, however, of the base communities is to see these tasks as *ministries*. They are ways in which a baptized lay person serves the community, and shares in the work of the Church. The work has dignity, because it is a part of Christ's mission to preach the gospel.

Some ministries are to serve the internal needs of the community. There needs to be someone to organize a meeting, someone to offer hospitality, someone to plan an agenda, someone to read from the Bible, someone to say a prayer, someone to lead the singing, someone to look after the purse, someone to coordinate the community with other communities or with the parish, someone for other members to turn to for a listening ear, and so on.

Other ministries are more outgoing, more missionary. One community I visited in Nicaragua, for example, took on a regular ministry of visiting the sick in a local hospital. They did not just visit those from their community, not even just those from their locality, but anyone who was there. The evening I came to the base community meeting, they were asking for contributions of children's garments for a very poor woman in the hospital who had difficulty clothing her family. Other ministries directed towards mission could include teaching literacy, or producing a newsletter,

---

[2] *Ecclesiogenesis*, p. 2. In Mendoza (ed.), *Church of the People: The Basic Christian Community Experience in the Philippines*, we read that out of eighteen base communities investigated, seventeen were initiated by the parish priest; in the one exception, the Diocesan Social Action Centre played a hand (p. 4).

or organizing social events for the wider community.

In the Philippines a common way of expressing the spread of ministries is through the abbreviation WESTY, which stands for Worship, Education, Service, Temporalities, Youth.

The tasks may sound small, but what is important is to recognize that everyone has something to offer, some contribution to make for the common good. Then everyone participates and everyone feels involved.

The other thing that is important is to recognize that there is a further dimension than just good group dynamics. This contribution for the common good is a ministry, a responsibility undertaken in the service of the Church, a way in which every person can be an apostle—laity as well as clergy.

When this basic lesson is learned and applied, we find there is no longer any shortage of ministers in the Church of Christ!

A cadre of thousands

Out of these base communities has arisen a cadre of thousands, those whom, in our theological language, we call 'ministers', that is, servants of the common interest. And so it came about that this Church, which was so lacking in priests, the classical agents of the traditional pastorate, that it had to bring them in from outside; this church sees rising up thousands of responsible ones, laypeople, poor and humble, generally young, who take care of every kind of service, including religious, ecclesiastical, and sacramental service, that the community needed . . .

That is not to say that we ever denied the specific value of the sacerdotal order[3] on the grounds of the flowering of lay ministries. But it is important to note that a pastorate to create priestly vocations is empty and even unhealthy unless it is preceded by a pastorate building the mission of the Christian people, taken in its entirety, with respect to the modern world.[4]

---

[3] i.e. the priesthood.
[4] Dominique Barbé, *Grace and Power*, p. 94.

Through the experience of ministries springing up anew according to need, and of ministers springing up ready and generous to serve the cause of the gospel, there comes also a sense of the Church being born afresh. This is what Church is all about, and it is happening today, in our world. Leonardo Boff enthusiastically explains why the basic Christian communities are such a rebirth of the Church, or *ecclesiogenesis*.

An ecclesiogenesis

As we have seen, they are genuine Church. Many functions, genuinely new ministries, appear in them — ministries of community coordination, of catechesis, of organizing the liturgy, of caring for the sick, of teaching people to read and write, of looking after the poor, and the like. All this is done in a deep spirit of communion, with a sense of joint responsibility and with an awareness of building and living actual Church. The best conceptualization of this experience is in the frequently heard expression, 'reinvention of the Church'. The Church is beginning to be born at the grassroots, beginning to be born at the heart of God's People.[5]

The next account is a well-known story about the beginnings of base community in Brazil. What is being talked of at this stage, back in the 1950s, is not yet basic ecclesial community, but rather a forerunner. Many observers hold that this development in the diocese of Barra do Pirai (state of Rio de Janeiro) was one of several convergent lines of experiment in Brazil, that eventually generated basic Christian communities.

Another of the other convergent lines was the Basic Education Movement (MEB[6]) and in particular the Natal radio-schools, in the state of Rio Grande do Norte. From 1958, the radio became an important means of educating people to cope with their problems of poverty, illness, ignorance, malnutrition, exploitation and injustice. An active group of priests played an important role in getting this going, and by 1963 there were 1,410 radio classes in the archdiocese of Natal alone, covering among other things literacy, consciousness-raising, catechesis, and broadcasting the bishop's Sunday mass as a focus for the worship of local groups. The MEB

---

[5] Leonardo Boff, *Ecclesiogenesis*, p. 23.
[6] *Movimento de Educação de Base.*

spread rapidly through the northeast and central west of the country, and was very much modelled on the ideas of Paulo Freire[7]. What this brought to base communities was the the idea of faith having consequences in social action and conscientization.

There are different views on exactly where and when the first base community was found. Frances O'Gorman reports that 'Some say the first base community was born in Nísia Floresta, in Rio Grande do Norte state; others say the place was Volta Redonda, Rio de Janeiro state. The date is the same: 1960.'[8] Dominique Barbé dates the birth of Brazilian basic ecclesial communities in 1968,[9] but most people would give an earlier date. For the Brazilian theologian Marcello Azevedo 'it is in the time-span 1963–67 that we can identify the first BECs in Brazil'.[10]

Whether or not the experiments in the early 1960s are called basic Christian community, they were given a paradoxical spur by the military coup of 1964. In the subsequent years of repressive government, meetings of all sorts fell under suspicion. Organizations from trade unions to university teachers' societies simply had to disband. The Church became the only place where people could meet and talk. Azevedo writes: 'In a political context where civil society as a whole was silenced by military or technocratic force, the Church was for many the voice of the voiceless.'[11]

The effect of this was to unite hierarchy and base, and give them a common sense of mission in the face of governmental injustice. The various branches of Catholic Action—including workers' movements and students' movements—drew closer together. (And we remember how important the 'see, judge, act' method of Catholic Action was to become for the base communities.)

Precise steps were now taken by the National Conference of Brazilian Bishops (CNBB): they launched the Joint Pastoral Plan (1965–70), which explicitly said: 'Our present parishes will or should be composed of various local communities and basic communities.' Then Medellín,[12] in 1968, gave more encouragement to what was going on, and the basic ecclesial communities multiplied a hundredfold.

So, out of the twin roots of lay catechists and MEB, fertilized by the Council, activated by the national crisis, and promoted by the

[7] See Appendix 2.
[8] *Base Communities in Brazil*, p. 28.
[9] *Grace and Power*, p. 92.
[10] *Basic Ecclesial Communities in Brazil*, p. 36.
[11] *Ibid.*, p. 65.
[12] See Appendix 1 and Appendix 3.

bishops, Brazil became the first, and still the greatest breeding ground for base communities.[13] By the mid-1980s estimates of the number of Brazilian base communities were shooting up from 50,000 to 100,000 and then again to 150,000. Everyone agrees that statistics are hard to come by: new communities begin and others come to an end even while you are counting.

We return now to how it all began in Barra do Pirai. This account captures a human story and shows that the shortage of priests was an important factor in the generation of the CEBs. Laypeople were invited to take on some of the work previously done by the clergy, and so local communities began a religious life of their own in the absence of the priest.

Christmas in Barra do Pirai

In 1956 Mgr Agnelo Rossi, then bishop of Barra do Pirai, started a missionary movement for the evangelization and 'welfare' of all areas of his vast diocese.

It began when an old woman said to the bishop during a pastoral visitation of her area, 'At Christmas the three Protestant churches were lit up and crowded. We could hear their hymn-singing . . . and our Catholic church, closed, was in darkness . . . because we could not get a priest.' This challenge prompted some fundamental questions such as: If there are not any priests, does everything have to stop? Cannot anyone else do anything for the life of the Church community?

Thus people's catechists were formed, trained as community coordinators who in the name of the bishop gathered the people together to pray, to listen to the reading of the Word of God, and thus kept alive their consciousness of the ecclesial community in fraternal communion. In 1956 there were already 372 such catechists. 'They do all a layperson can do in the Church of God within present ecclesiastical discipline. At the very least the catechist assembles the people once a week and gives catechetical instruction. Normally he says daily prayers with them . . . On Sundays and holy days he

---

[13] For the origins of CEBs in Brazil, cf. Azevedo, Chapter 1.

> *gathers together people who live far from the church for*
> *the "Sunday without Mass", or the "Mass without a*
> *priest", or the "Catholic service", and gets the people to*
> *accompany collectively in spirit the Mass which the*
> *parish priest is celebrating in the distant mother-church.*
> *He recites with the people morning and night prayers,*
> *novenas, litanies, May or June devotions, etc.* "[14]

The last passage showed what a central role was played by lay ministries when base communities began in Brazil. In Central America, San Miguelito in Panama was a key forerunner, influencing the spread of basic Christian communities into other Central American countries.[15] In the early history of San Miguelito, as in Brazil, we see the crucial importance of developing lay ministries.

The San Miguelito area began with an invasion of people from the country, looking for somewhere to live, and the bishop invited three priests from Chicago to set up a new parish. The priests based their early work with the people on helping them to explore their present situation.[16] What had motivated them to leave the piece of land on which their parents and grandparents had lived, in order to come to this place. What were they *really* looking for? 'To put this question to people and make them come to the realization that they were looking for something great, not just for something good, but for something great . . . that was really the basis for the church in San Miguelito at that time.'[17]

In the early years there was much reliance on funds from Chicago. With this money, a number of paid catechists were employed to carry out the Church's work. But after a few years the funding came to an end, and the parish was thrown back onto its own resources. This might have seemed a disaster at the time, but in fact it reaped a rich harvest. The people now had to organize themselves, and six years later, there were eighty basic ecclesial communities functioning.[18]

[14] José Marins in *Concilium* (1975) (4), quoting from *Revista Eclesiástica Brasileira* 17 (1957), pp. 731–7. This is also found in *International Review of Mission* 68 (1979), p. 271. See also Boff, *Ecclesiogenesis*, pp. 3–4.
[15] See also p. 61.
[16] What Latin Americans would call the **reality**: see Appendix 1.
[17] Donald Headley, a later parish priest in San Miguelito, speaking in 1972. See note 19 below.
[18] This story comes from José Marins at a workshop in Birmingham in 1990.

Speaking in an interview, Donald Headley, a priest in San Miguelito, describes how the most unlikely people began to be liberated by the challenge they found in the base communities.

Come and see

Donald Headley: *It's interesting how many people say the same thing they said to the Lord: 'Where do you live? What are you really all about? Where do you come from?' It's interesting sometimes the stuttering people who say that, the people that cannot speak well, and the people who have difficulty in expressing themselves and are not quite sure of themselves. When they ask that question, and somebody says 'Well come and see', all of a sudden they begin to speak, and they begin to walk in a different way, and they begin to take on themselves the attributes of prophet and teacher that Paul talked about so much.*

Donald Headley reports in the same interview on an early event that stimulated lay ministries and helped to overcome the assumption that only the clergy had a ministry.[19]

Forget about the diaconate

Donald Headley: *A sizeable number of people were trained as deacons. The bishop took the reports and petitions to Rome—which were very formal, very definite. He lost them all somewhere between here and Rome. Anyway they never arrived where they were supposed to go. There were six or seven copies and he lost them all. After waiting and waiting, the men finally said, 'Let's cut this out. Let's have a lay ministry. Forget about the diaconate.' So we set them apart and they just got on with the job.*

By 1972, when Donald Headley was speaking, there were 250 people involved in ministry. A small, working-class team of about six priests and nine laity had the task of ministering to the

[19] This interview is available in the Basic Christian Communities Resource Centre, Scottish Churches House, Dunblane, and the second extract also appears in Ian Fraser, *The Fire Runs*, pp. 16ff.

ministers. One day, reports Donald, the lay members called the priests to a meeting and said 'This can't go on any more. Things aren't going too well and you are liable to be thrown out tomorrow. So then what? So we are going to take over.' The priests replied, 'Hey, congratulations! That's the best thing we've heard in a long time.' 'And', commented Donald, 'as far as the bishops are concerned we are the pastors, but really we are the technical assistants.'

What it feels like to be a simple, poor person, and at the same time called by Christ to be a lay minister, is described here by Carlos Zarco Mera, an animator of a basic ecclesial community in Mexico City.

Jesus called me

Today, for instance, I have a meeting in which we come together as representatives of communities from different parts of the city; there are, of course, other complications that arise from time to time.

I wish to make it quite clear that all of these meetings are necessary in order to ensure that our work is progressing according to the Gospel and that it answers the needs of our people. In these coordinators' meetings we evaluate and examine our work in the light of the word of God in order to improve our work; it is quite a responsibility to be in charge of a community and we have to serve with all our strength and all our minds.

In meetings with my own community I have the responsibility of ensuring that the aim of the meeting is accomplished. Of course, I don't do everything. At any meeting, we share out the various activities, for instance, the time-keeper, the one who prepares the prayer, the one in whose house we meet . . . etc. Each week, we take turns in doing these things. I am acting as animator for the present but, through time, this task will also become someone else's responsibility.

When there are specific things going on in the neighbourhood or when there is a particular problem to be solved, we all take our share of the task in hand.

We call all of these tasks a form of service because that is precisely what they are . . .

> *In the Bible there is passage that reads: 'Then Jesus went up into the hills and called to him those whom he desired; and they came to him . . .' (Mark 3:13). I sincerely believe that Jesus called me, that he chose me and that I have given him an affirmative response; of course, this means that I have to be pure in heart, I often fall into sin and I know that I am a sinner but I believe that, even so, Jesus still calls me.*[20]

ALL ARE EQUAL IN THE BASE COMMUNITY

When we realize that everyone has a ministry, of one kind or another, then the equality of Christians becomes much more real. No longer is there a division of those who minister and those who are ministered to, of active and passive. Instead there is a genuine body of Christ, in which every member has a role to play.

It is easy to pay lip-service to this idea, and pay no attention to it in practice. We may talk about 'the servants of the servants of God' but, as Ian Fraser once pointed out, that should imply servants' wages and servants' quarters. Instead we often find the language of service misused to legitimate and excuse the privileges of a very separate, clerical class.

In the base communities it is different: the priest, the bishop and the theologian are treated and behave as brothers and equals of the laity.

Here is an incident from the Seventh Interecclesial Assembly of CEBs of Brazil, which I witnessed.

The gift of a shell

> *Perhaps the most moving stories were of the suffering of the Indians. 'My name is Palm Tree', said an Indian chief, 'and we must be like palm trees: when we are cut and burnt down we must put out new shoots and grow green and strong again.' A letter from the representatives of Indian nations was read which brought 'a message of sadness and hope.*

[20] Concilium 176 (1984), pp. 65–6.

*Our young people no longer speak our language. We
are forbidden to meet and talk about our problems.
The police are always in our areas, trying to create
division among us. We are losing our knowledge of
natural medicines . . . But we hope you will help us
and fight with us for our common liberation. Poor
people always help poor people, and when we have
won back our lands we promise to help other poor
elsewhere, for our God is the same as yours.'*

*The Indian representatives presented a gift of a
huge and beautiful shell, explaining that since they
no longer had land they had to give something they
had fished up from the water. The gift was for Dom
Mauro Morelli, who was host to the Assembly, but
unfortunately it turned out he was not present at
that moment. Who could stand in for him, at such a
moving and delicate juncture? Some diocesan
official, perhaps?*

*In the place of the bishop, a delegation was brought
forward of . . . kitchen staff. It was explained that
amongst them were descendants of Indian, African
and Portuguese stock. As a multi-racial group of
representatives of the Brazilian people, they solemnly,
in the bishop's name, accepted the shell from the
persecuted and marginalized Indians. Only amongst
basic Christian communities would such an
imaginative and apt solution be thought of, for it
was a gesture that really conveyed with conviction
the message: 'We are all equal here.'*[21]

This next story is a really testing one. Three priests in the Philippines, including the author, Niall O'Brien, had been arrested and
imprisoned on a trumped-up charge of murder, together with six
of their lay leaders from the base communities. After negotiations,
the three priests were released on bail—but only after a long and
fierce argument because they did not want to leave without their
lay colleagues, and their bishop had to exert enormous pressure to
persuade them to come out.

Some months later, the priests could no longer bear the injustice
of their privileged position:

[21] This is expanded from my report in *The Tablet* (5 August 1989).

Back to Bacolod Jail

*I spoke to Brian and Itik, and they agreed that the
time was ripe to hand in our privilege of house arrest
and join our leaders, who all this time had been in
that fetid hole called Bacolod Provincial Jail.*

*But how would the bishop react? We planned it
carefully. We sent a telegram to President Marcos,
and Brian and Itik slipped their guards. I brought
mine with me, and we drove to the bishop's house.
It was three in the afternoon. He was still at* siesta.
*We waited impatiently, putting our ear to the door
to hear if the shower was going. Finally we heard it,
and a few minutes later we entered.*

*One of the greatest gifts a priest can have is a
bishop who is* simpatico. *Bishop Fortich was this,
and for that reason we did not want to hurt his
feelings or go against him. However, we now felt we
must join the others. The telegram had already been
sent. What if he disagreed?*

*He welcomed us and told us to pull up three
chairs. He guessed it was something important. We
had decided that it would be Itik who would break
the news, but I almost regretted that because it took
Itik an age to get the words out. He went round and
round, till finally he abruptly said: 'Monsignor, we
are going back to jail.' The bishop puffed his pipe
and smiled: 'You're probably doing the right thing.'
We were overcome with emotion and we all leapt up
and threw our arms about him. It was such a relief
that an end was in sight to the shame of us being
out and our companions being in.*[22]

Just as priests are equal to laity, so too are bishops. Leonardo Boff
winningly points out: 'Evangelization is a two-way street. The
bishop evangelizes the people, and the people evangelize the
bishop. Otherwise who evangelizes the bishop? Who sees to his
salvation?'[23]

The next extract comes from a Pastoral Message on basic ecclesial
communities, signed by fifteen Mexican bishops.

---

[22] *Revolution from the Heart*, pp. 284–5.
[23] *Ecclesiogenesis*, p. 40.

Bishops are evangelized by the people

*In order to continue advancing the life of God and
of the Church in the CEBs, and for them to be able
to overcome these obstacles adequately, the CEBs
need our pastoral accompaniment as bishops, in
accordance with our charism and our episcopal duties.*

*In this accompaniment of the CEBs we ourselves,
evangelizers, have been evangelized by the poor. Our
closeness to them and our relationship with them have
made us feel more vividly than ever the project of God,
and also the project of death which opposes it.*[24]

And in this passage, Aloisio Lorscheider—who is a Cardinal as well
as an Archbishop—describes how his episcopal style changed after
he was transferred to the diocese of Fortaleza in north-east Brazil.

A bishop learns to adopt a simple life-style

*In a short while it became clear to me that my
episcopal ministry would be exercised in a different
way. I would always be an extra member of a
community, with my own special responsibility in it,
but without seeing myself or being seen as the head
of that community, as superior to it; rather, as a
member of the community vested with Christ's
exousia for the sacrament of order. I should be there
only to serve at the moment when they felt a need
for the service I could give, or when I felt, in the
spirit of fraternal charity, that I could be a help to
them on their way. I was no longer the teacher or
instructor, but one animator among a lot of other
animators . . .*

*To take the allegory of the Good Shepherd (John
10) as an illustration, I no longer saw myself as
someone leading my flock, but as someone walking
in the middle of the flock, together with the flock,
without for a moment hiding the figure of the one
true shepherd, Jesus Christ . . .*

[24] *The Base Ecclesial Communities, Church in Movement*, 2.6, 7. It was
signed at Guadalajara, Jalisco, on 7 April 1989.

The way the poor, religious people of the communities regard their bishop is something that never fails to make an impression on me. How they desire the presence of the bishop! The bishop's presence at their meetings, in their daily lives, is what they appreciate most. They see it as an enormous support, a stimulus that leaves them happy, full of courage and enthusiasm. The bishop can spend the whole day at one of their meetings without opening his mouth; his presence alone is everything to them. Nevertheless, it does sometimes happen that they openly ask the bishop for his opinion, and he does have perfect freedom to intervene when he thinks it convenient or necessary.

For me, pastoral visitations have become far easier to carry out. I no longer need to prepare lists or catechisms. Everything springs from the lives of these poor and deeply religious people. Their feeling for faith is a reality one can touch with one's hands.

Today I also see the problem of vocations in the Church in a different light. The real problem is how to gather people together in small, living apostolic communities, not how to herd them into seminaries and convents. The small ecclesial communities will produce the various ministries and services the People of God need. There is a whole new structure of ecclesial experience coming to life. The problem now is how to form these ministers and servers in the spirit of Christ and his Church.

Finally, this new way of being bishop based on very concrete contact with the communities of the poor and religious people leads the bishop to a simpler life-style, making him feel the need to identify himself more and more with the Poor Christ and the poor people (os pobres), avoiding anything that can give the impression of greatness or ruling status. The bishop becomes a brother among brothers.

These, then, are some aspects of the life of the communities that have taught me how to be a bishop today in the Third World—and perhaps also in the First.[25]

[25] Concilium 176, pp. 48–9.

PEOPLE ARE CALLED TO DIFFERENT MINISTRIES

How do you decide who takes what ministry? Essentially it is a matter of balancing up what needs to be done against what people have to offer. Different people are gifted in different ways, so it is not just a matter of circulating every task, for that may not be in the interests of the community.

It is worth pointing this out, because on more than one occasion I have come across communities in the first world that were so anxious about being egalitarian and avoiding elitism, that no one ever took responsibility for anything. Every task had to be equally shared among all, so that, for example, chairing the meeting was never done by the same person more than once; or choosing music for the liturgy could not be planned as a whole because no single person was allowed to suggest more than one hymn. By that approach, the communities hope to ensure that no one becomes too powerful, but they also have a lot of chaos. And usually there is one powerful person to whom the rules of circulating power do not apply (invariably this is the priest). If there were not, probably nothing at all would ever take place.

This is egalitarianism taken to excess. There are many ways of affirming that everyone is equal without insisting that everyone does the same tasks. 'All are equal, but not all do everything', says Leonardo Boff.[26]

This excessive egalitarianism also blocks off the initiative of the Spirit, that distributes different gifts to different people. St Paul calls these charisms. And so, if a person has a gift for a particular kind of work, we can see the prior action of God at work, preparing a person to be ready to exercise a ministry.

Leonardo Boff summarizes here the scriptural basis for charisms.

The charisms of the Spirit

The presence of the Spirit is made visible by a 'plurality of gifts' or 'charisms' (1 Cor 12:5). In Pauline terminology, these are simply services which he enumerates at great length (1 Cor 12:8–10; Rom 12:6–7; Eph 4:11–12). Some of these services–gifts attend to the collective needs of the community,

[26] *Ecclesiogenesis*, p. 27.

> *such as the service of mercy (Rom 12:8) or that of
> exhortation (Rom 12:8), healing and miracles (1 Cor
> 12:9), while others meet structural needs such as
> teaching, leadership, discernment of Spirits (1 Cor
> 12:10; Eph 4:11; Rom 12:8), all of which demand
> constant attention . . .*
>
> *Paul makes charism the structuring element of the
> community . . . For Paul charism means simply the
> concrete function that each person exercises within
> the community for the good of all . . .*
>
> *The routine as well as the extraordinary is covered
> by the term* charism. *True charism blossoms where
> individuals place all that they are, all that they have,
> and all they can do at the service of God and
> neighbour. Their gifts come from the Spirit and
> become fruitful, like the talents in the gospel.*[27]

The vocation to a particular ministry does not exist in a vacuum: there must also be a need for that kind of work to be done, so that it is truly an act of service to the community. But we cannot always trust individuals to discern their callings for themselves.

Some people are afraid to be presumptuous, and hesitate to put themselves forward. They need encouragement from the community, so that the call of the community activates the charism they have.

Others are the opposite, making the community serve their needs rather than making their needs serve the community. They may take on ministries that are not wanted, or they may hog ministries that other people could do better. They need a gentle steering hand that ensures that the community comes first, without damping the spirits of the energetic and generous.

For example, a secret ballot for the coordinator can often be a good idea. Otherwise there can sometimes be a risk, on the one hand, of offending a pushy person who has offered his or her services, and on the other, of having members drift away because they do not like how things are being run but do not want to say so.

When the Spirit gives a charism to a person, and the community confirms that it is the right moment to exercise that charism, then we can begin to speak of vocation. It is God who calls us, but who is to say when a call comes from God? When both the community

---

[27] *Church, Charism and Power*, pp. 156–8.

and the individual agree on the exercising of a ministry, then we can be reasonably confident that there is a genuine vocation.

It could be objected that, even if this understanding may possibly be applied to lay ministries, it is in no way implemented when it comes to the clergy. Candidates for the priesthood generally put themselves forward, rather than being suggested by the community. A vocation to the clerical ministries is understood predominantly as a subjective sense of feeling called, and this call is sometimes felt by people who would not otherwise be put forward by the community as being gifted with the charism of leadership. Meanwhile many people whom the community would like to suggest are ruled out in advance, either because of their marital status or because of their sex. There is a great deal in these criticisms, and the next passage from Dominique Barbé makes a plea for change on just these grounds.

Nonetheless, there is not a total incompatibility between the two approaches. However insistent an individual is that he 'has a vocation' he can be turned down by the bishop or the seminary if they have doubts about his vocation, so it is not an entirely subjective matter. The Church does have a say, though at a higher level than the local community.

Perhaps in the past too many unsuitable people have been allowed through the seminary system, because of the overall scarcity of priests. Recently we have been seeing some problems arising from this laxity, and a number of Catholic priests are even serving prison sentences for criminal offences.

Certainly there is need for reform. And this reform should be based on a theology that links not just lay ministries but all ministries more firmly to the charisms that come from God and are confirmed by the community.

Here is what Dominique Barbé has to say on the role of the local community in recognizing a vocation.

Vocation in the early Church

As long as there is lacking such an ecclesial fullness through which the people of God can make its voice heard, in an explicit manner, at the moment when important decisions are to be made, just so long will there continue to be a kind of contradiction between the Church of base communities, which is born from the people, and the Church that names *priests, bishops, and nuncios from on high and* sends *them to communities. That was not the custom of the primitive Church. Its equilibrium was more complex.*

On the one hand, communities, whether local as in the form of a parish or a diocese, were recognized as having the right of nominating their candidate to join the presbyterate or the episcopacy. There did not exist the concept of the sending by religious authority of a pastor, whether priest or bishop, who was in some sense external to the community . . .

But on the other hand, the local bishop had to come and confirm or reject this choice, and only the bishop could ordain the one proposed by the people. For it was recognized that no community ever formed a separate whole, closed in on itself, without any possibility of intervention by other churches and the religious authority.

The same procedure held as regards the episcopate; the people had an active voice. It will be remembered that many bishops were elevated to their office, sometimes against their will, by popular acclamation: by the cry, 'Ambrose, bishop!' 'Augustine, bishop!' This was the way Ambrose was elected bishop of Milan; Augustine, of Hippo . . .

On the other hand—and herein lies the extent of the primitive equilibrium—never was a bishop (or a priest) consecrated or ordained by the person's own community. The bishops of the three neighbouring cities came to verify whether or not the bishop-elect held the catholic and apostolic faith, and possessed the qualities of a pastor. They had the power of refusing a candidate . . .

Thus communion was assured; and the twin dangers of bureaucratic centralism and of sectarianism were avoided . . .

Today matters are exactly the opposite: the religious authority names and sends, the one elected 'feels' the vocation, the community has hardly anything to say at all . . . A certain practice in the base community is contradicted by a different practice on the level of the universal Church in the West. This contradiction, in our opinion, accounts for the uneasy reaction from the structure each time an attempt is made to improve the status of the base community.[28]

THE HIERARCHY HAS A PLACE AS THE MINISTRY OF UNITY

We have seen that equality does not mean everyone does the same tasks, but allows for different ministries. And we have seen that bishops learn from, and are evangelized by, the laity. It follows, then, that there is a place for hierarchy in a Church of base communities, however off-putting the associations of the word 'hierarchy' may have become. Indeed, there is a need for hierarchy. But the hierarchy may need to look more carefully at their own ministry, in order to exercise it better. There is much need for reform.

Certainly, in practice, the people of the third-world base communities love their bishops, even if they are sometimes hurt by them.

Leonardo Boff explains here, clearly and convincingly, why hierarchy is not abolished in the theology of basic ecclesial community. He is not for a moment implying, of course, that the hierarchical function in the Catholic Church today is actually exercised in the way he suggests it ought to be.

The charism of unity

What would the Church be if there were a multiplicity of charisms without any order among them? How would all the members constitute one body, if there were no one to see that the charisms were exercised for the common good? . . .

Power structures in the Church do not necessarily violate its charismatic nature. Power can be a charism, as long as it serves everyone and is an instrument for building justice in the community . . .

There is a charism, one among many but of prime importance, which is that of being responsible for harmony among the many and diverse charisms. This charism is proper to those who occupy positions of leadership within the community. We commonly call it the hierarchy . . .

[28] Grace and Power, pp. 114–16.

The specific function of the hierarchy (those who are in leadership roles) is not accumulation but integration, making way for unity and harmony among the various services so that any single one does not trip up, drown out, or downplay another. From this comes the immediate subordination of the members to those in the hierarchy. However, the hierarchy does not exist to subordinate but rather to nourish the spirit of brotherhood and sisterhood and of unity. The charism of unity implies all other charisms, such as dialogue, patience, listening, serenity, knowledge of the human heart with its desire for power and self-affirmation. This hierarchical function is carried out by the coordinator of a local ecclesial community, by the bishop in his diocese, and by the Pope in the universal Church.

Due to the charism of unity, there are those who preside at the celebrations of the community, those who are primarily responsible for orthodox doctrine, and for the order of charity. It is particularly necessary for these persons to discern the spirit of the community and to watch that all charisms retain their nature as charism, in service for the good of the community.[29]

What Boff presents is essentially a Catholic view of Church communion, with the Pope as the overall focus of unity for the whole Church, and the bishops acting as overseers, enabling the local churches to be in unity not only with each other but also with the other dioceses all over the world.

But not all the people who are interested in base communities are Catholic. In fact there are many signs that, in the first world today, Protestants from the mainline denominations are pushing ahead faster than Catholics with exploring how base communities can be implemented. For those who do not see a world-wide institutional unity as a necessary part of what it means to be Church, will not the understanding of basic ecclesial community inevitably be slightly different?

Inevitably it will, but as with all ecumenical questions, the modifications often turn out to be more minor than we think at first. Mainline Protestants also have a sense of universal Church,

[29] *Church, Charism and Power*, pp. 160–4.

without seeing the Pope as symbol of that universality. They too can put a high premium on communion, and defend the necessity of institutional union, without accepting the same conditions of communion or living under the same type of institution as a Catholic does. But there is a spread of views, and it is also possible for some from Protestant Church backgrounds to sit much more loosely to any international institutional structure.

Among those who are interested in base communities, then, there can be quite different and even contradictory understandings. The differences in conception concern how much institutional unity is necessary to the base communities, whether the hierarchy have a place in them, how free individual communities are to celebrate the sacraments of the Church without reference to the authority of the wider Church, and so on.

What one might call the more anti-institutional concept of base communities is more common in the first world, and especially in Europe — even in countries with large Catholic populations like Italy, Spain and Holland — where some small groups, desperately frustrated with the hierarchy, are feeling a need to go ahead on their own.

This book draws its ecclesiology principally from Catholic, third-world theologians. But we must be clear that the term 'basic Christian community' is used in different ways, and be ready to recognize the different ecclesiological assumptions when we meet them.

The difference is well expressed and contrasted in the following two extracts. The first passage is from *The Fire Runs* by Ian Fraser — a Church of Scotland minister, formerly working for the World Council of Churches, who has visited more communities in both first and third worlds than anyone else I know. In this passage he explains clearly and forcefully his objections to hierarchy:

A few swallows do not make a summer

*If the people of God keep their nerve, hierarchies
have had their day . . .*

*Of course there are hierarchies and hierarchies. Are
there some which effectively release the people of
God into their joyful task? . . . If the people of God
are released by a form of leadership we are no longer
justified in calling that hierarchy. For hierarchy
indicates a sacred caste group who bear rule over
others and make abuse of power to protect their own
interests and their own positions. Wherever you find*

*hierarchies you find manipulation, restrictive
practices, administrative and financial pressures . . .*

*The action of a man like Dom Hélder Câmara and
his leadership in the hierarchy in the Recife area of
Brazil may offer fresh encouragement for the future
of this form of Church government. But he and
those who join with him still form only a very small
and unrepresentative proportion of the official
leadership in Brazil. A few swallows do not make a
summer . . .*

*Coming down to earth, what alternative do we
have to hierarchies or bureaucratistic equivalents?
What alternative pattern is desirable?*

*There is no one alternative pattern. Patterns are
developing all over the world. We are back in times
like that of the early Church. The volcanic fires of
the gospel are changing out of recognition what were
familiar ecclesiastical landscapes. The most obvious
thing is what is not being given attention—we must
sit at the feet of the world Church and discover how
God is disposing his forces . . .*

*Alternative forms of ministry are sprouting
everywhere in the world Church.*[30]

The dilemma opened up by Ian Fraser could be summed up in the
question: how far can you go? Does developing lay ministries lead
to abandoning ordained ministries?

In contrast to the previous passage, the next extract shows a more
'Catholic' approach, more typical of third-world thinking. It comes
from Ian Fraser's interview with Daniel Jensen, in Guatemala.[31]

Not an underground Church

Daniel Jensen: *In Europe the understanding of the
basic Christian community has been one of
underground Church, Church that is in defiance, at
times, or at least in conflict with the hierarchy,*

[30] pp. 112–5.
[31] This interview can be found in the Basic Christian Communities
Resource Centre at Scottish Churches House, Dunblane. See also pp. 11
and 46 above.

whereas in Latin America basic Christian community is not that at all. The basic Christian community is a small cell of the Church, a clone of the Church if you will, that grows only in so far as it is connected with the hierarchy and follows the main stream of the Church coming from Jesus through the apostles down to our day. We speak of basic Christian community in English, whereas in Spanish we speak of basic ecclesial communities. Any community which cuts its ties with the hierarchy loses its validity and loses its right to call itself ecclesial. With that, they can become basic community but they are no longer basic ecclesial communities, and for us that is a very important distinction. If we lose our ties, if we lose our connection with the hierarchy, I find that we of the communities tend to become weak because our strength comes from our connection with Jesus and that connection, for us, comes through the hierarchy of the Church.

Ian Fraser: *Well I think you would find quite a bit of contrast and challenge from some European areas with regard to that position.*

These are contentious issues, and it is important not to fudge them. There *are* different understandings of base community, and unless that is recognized there will be much confusion and hurt. For example, some first-world people of a more anti-institutional viewpoint can assume that the Catholic base communities in the third world are half-way along the road to shaking off the repressive hand of Roman authority, and poised to celebrate the eucharist on their own terms. This is a tragic misunderstanding.

Worse, to see the third-world base communities in this light is a new form of European cultural imperialism, because it assumes that they have not fully worked out the logical consequences of the path they have begun on. It assumes that there is an inconsistency about the base communities, which have gone so far in finding their own feet and taking their own initiatives, and which yet ultimately allow themselves to be frustrated and blocked by an uncomprehending hierarchy.

A first-world attitude of this sort deals a grave blow to the efforts of third-world base communities to find greater recognition and encouragement from Rome. No wonder the Vatican is suspicious of base communities when some of the examples it sees around itself in Italy and the rest of Europe seem to take an anti-institutional stand as a defining characteristic.

Repeatedly the third-world base communities reply that they are not a movement within the Church, but the Church in movement. The base communities reform, rejuvenate, restructure the institution in order to recentre it on Christ. They do not leave the institution on one side in the belief that they can recentre themselves on Christ all by themselves.

PASTORAL AGENTS ARE ESSENTIAL AS LEAVEN

A very common misunderstanding about base communities is that, because they are grassroots groups which operate from the bottom up, therefore they spring up without anyone from above intervening. The truth is that spontaneous combustion simply does not happen: there has to be a spark to light the fire. Or, to change the metaphor, dough does not rise unless someone kneads yeast (or leaven) into it. 'The kingdom of heaven is like leaven which a woman took and hid in three measures of flour, till it was all leavened' (Matthew 13:33).

So we should not over-emphasize the bottom-up element to the exclusion of all else. There is a two-way movement. From the bottom there rises up what Dominique Barbé called 'a cadre of thousands'. From the top there must be the preparation of an environment in which people have room to grow.

And there must be an actual personal contact to set the ball rolling. There must be someone who opens people's eyes and broadens their horizons, who helps others to understand what basic Christian community means and how to go about it. We call that person a 'pastoral agent', meaning someone who 'acts' pastorally. They are like a raising 'agent' in baking.

There are many kinds of ministries that can come under the general heading of 'pastoral agent'. Anyone who is a parish priest or sister is a pastoral agent. Anyone who is a community co-ordinator or animator or catechist is a pastoral agent. A pastoral agent, in short, is anyone, clerical or religious or lay, who takes pastoral initiatives. This personal invitation, to which people respond, is like the story at the beginning of John's gospel, when Andrew finds Simon, and invites him, and Philip finds Nathanael, and invites him (John 1:41, 45).

The theologian Marcello Azevedo points out from his experience in Brazil, that no basic Christian communities would have arisen without the crucial role of pastoral agents.

Left to themselves, the people would not have gotten there

The BECs did not arise spontaneously out of the base, out of the common people composing them. They were the result of the consciousness-raising activity of clergy and religious, who were helping the people to see real elements of their life and historical situation. The main reason for their rapid growth lies in the correspondence between the elements introjected by pastoral agents and the concrete needs of the people. To deny one of the two terms would be to succumb to a partial view of the situation . . .

Left to themselves, the people would not have gotten there. Even after a good start has been made, much of the further development and course of BEC life depends on the training of lay leaders. That training is largely given by priests and religious, or by lay leaders who agree with the objectives and programs proposed by the clergy for the BECs.[32]

Niall O'Brien tells of his great relief when some of his lay community leaders became able—as a result of a training course—to act more effectively as pastoral agents, so taking much pressure off him as priest.

The return from the Community Life Seminar

Now those leaders were coming back.

Their arrival back from Mindanao caused great excitement. The wives and husbands were waiting in the convento, and soon after the leaders arrived I could see the change. Until then I had been used to making out the agenda and presiding over the

---

[32] *Basic Ecclesial Communities in Brazil: The Challenge of a New Way of Being Church*, pp. 35, 82.

*meetings, but now they no longer waited for me to
start things. After supper they divided up tasks
among the group: prayer-leader, minute-taker,
song-leader, discussion-moderator. They made an
agenda and asked me whether I had anything to
add. Then they set up a priority for the items to be
discussed and allotted a cutoff time. Next came a
reading from the Scriptures, followed by a short
sharing of reflections and then into the first topic,
which turned out to be nothing less than setting up
a proper leadership course for our Christian
community members. They were going to attempt
the ambitious plan of echoing in the Christian
communities of Tabugon the six-week course they
had received in Ozamis City, but they would do it
in a ten-day seminar! I realized immediately the
logistics this would involve—communicating with all
the communities, organizing them to collect the
food from each community to support those
members who would be going, and so on.*

*Until now I would never have gone off before a
meeting was over. I couldn't—the meeting was me. I
would stay on, hurrying them up impatiently, saying
that they were taking too long to get to the point,
and coming in too often with the solution. But this
time I went off to bed and left them still planning.
I felt a very rich man.*[33]

---

[33] Revolution from the Heart, pp. 138–9.

1

Terms from liberation theology

INTRODUCTION

Within Latin America, basic ecclesial communities and liberation theology have grown up side by side, the one supporting the other.

A Church of basic ecclesial communities is the sort of Church that emerges from liberation theology. You cannot have liberation theology without the impetus to reconstruct the Church along base-community lines.

At the same time, liberation theology has grown out of the base communities. The theology of poor and simple people, which is first expressed in the privacy of the base communities, comes to be called liberation theology when it is more widely published, articulated through the voices of trained theologians.

Just as action feeds into reflection and reflection again into action (as we shall see again in Appendix 2, on Freire), so too base communities have fed into liberation theology, and liberation theology has fed into base communities.

We can even say that base communities are not just a branch of liberation theology — their ecclesiology, as distinct from their Christology or their soteriology. More than that, base communities are the ecclesial context in which liberation theology can occur. And so I decided I could not conclude this book without some kind of a key to the thought-world of liberation theology.

There is something of a dilemma over how you use the term 'liberation theology'. Is it, strictly speaking, only Latin American? Or should we include the theology coming out of other third-world countries, and out of marginalized communities in the first world? Because the Latin Americans have formed a distinct and important school of theology, which has a certainty priority at the present time in shaping theological thinking all over the world, I have concentrated this Appendix predominantly, but by no means exclusively, on Latin American liberation theology.

Most people know liberation theology is controversial, but when they try to study it they often find themselves put off by what can sound a dense and puzzling new language. This is particularly baffling when they know that liberation theology is supposed to be a theology of the poor, based on experience, and instead they find it turgid and technical to read. Leonardo Boff may have said, after his studies in Europe and before his return home, 'When I get back to Brazil I am going to write the kind of theology people can read the way they read a newspaper',[1] but it is doubtful whether he has succeeded, or indeed whether any of his fellow theologians have managed to attain that kind of readability.

The problem is that too many people attempt to get into liberation theology through reading books, because they are used to getting into the European theological tradition through reading books. But liberation theology is more of an oral tradition than a written one, emerging as it does from the experience of the communities. To get the authentic flavour of liberation theology, you need to meet people and hear how they talk. You need to experience how they do theology in a context, responding to actual situations. This sometimes comes across in books, but it often does not.

I found liberation theology came to life when I began to hear liberation theologians speak. I met the Brazilian J. B. Libânio at a colloquium in Paris, and was deeply impressed by his forceful commitment and his evident intellectual incisiveness. By any standards he was a very good thinker. And as a liberation theologian he was clearly speaking not just for himself but as a representative of a whole body of opinion that was behind him, and that was being constantly worked and shaped as a joint venture.

Then I met Jon Sobrino, a theologian from El Salvador, many times, when he spent a term in Oxford lecturing on the God of the poor. The ideas of liberation theology sprang into life through the

---

[1] Quoted by Harvey Cox in *The Silencing of Leonardo Boff*, p. 27.

spoken word. Here was a theologian who cared about what he was saying, who *communicated* rather than lectured, who could set hearts on fire and change lives. But he was not just a moving preacher — he was also evidently extremely intelligent, and steeped in a deep understanding of the tradition of the Church.

Later I went to Brazil, and met a whole group of world-famous liberation theologians, who were putting their skills at the service of the Seventh Interecclesial Assembly of Basic Ecclesial Communities at Duque de Caxias. Again I was struck by the power of this way of doing theology — not telling people what was what, but using their expertise and their gifts of exposition to shape the contributions of the conference into an effective and coordinated whole. I was struck by how simply and clearly they spoke — quite differently in many cases from the way they would express themselves in writing. And I was struck by how much they lived their faith, showing themselves to be brothers and sisters and friends of all who were there — whether local representatives from rural communities, or European observers who did not speak Portuguese.

Some have had this experience of excitement through reading books of liberation theology, but it is less common. Alfred T. Hennelly recounts that 'my own acquaintance with this theology began in the late sixties when I came across some writings of the Peruvian theologian Gustavo Gutiérrez. The words of Keats from some forgotten course flashed before me — "then felt I like some watcher of the skies, when a new planet swims into his ken" — and I have followed this movement with great interest in the intervening years.'[2]

More often the sense of discovery comes through a person-to-person experience, as with this vivid account by James Pitt of a visit to the *barrio* of São Mateus in São Paulo:

> *It was a small group of mothers, eight in all, meeting in one of their houses. The catechist, an American sister, was taking them through a catechetics programme that had been developed by basic church communities in the sector to help prepare children for first communion. The programme covered 30 themes, and every two weeks their mothers would study one theme as a group, teach their own children individually, and then evaluate it as a group.*

[2] *Liberation Theology: a Documentary History*, Preface, p. xiii.

I went to the meeting, hoping it would be interesting, but little prepared for an experience that would teach me more about liberation theology than anything I had heard or read to date . . .

The theme that fortnight was that Jesus was born poor and humble and shares our life, and the question was 'Why?' The women present were all poor. None had had much formal education. Most were migrants from rural areas. All knew real hardship. They could easily identify with a poor family on the move whose baby had been born in a stable. Indeed a one-minute reading of St Luke's account of the nativity provoked a one-hour discussion of the injustices, humiliations and hardships that the mothers themselves experienced.

They discussed the terrible health services available in the area and how a local woman's baby had been born while she was waiting in the queue to see the doctor (the baby died). They swapped accounts of having to wait in shops while better dressed people were served first and how as domestic servants they were treated without respect by their mistresses. They talked of the high price of food in the local shops . . .

After an hour the catechist put the question 'Why did Jesus choose to be born poor and humble?'

'Maybe', said one woman, a mother of ten of whom three had died and only two were working, 'maybe it was to show these rich people that we are important too.'

A ripple of excitement went through the room. Was God really such a clear statement about their *humanity? About* their *rights as people? The discussion progressed, but with an electric charge in the air. Half an hour later, a young woman said 'I think we still haven't got the right answer to the first question!' A complete hush. 'I think', she went on,* 'that God chose his son to be born like us so that we can realise that we are important, It is not just to show the bosses. It's to show *us* too!'

And suddenly I saw what it means to say that the Gospel has the power to set people free, that the Good News to the poor is a message of liberation.[3]

---

[3] Good News to All, pp. 8–9.

If we are dealing with a predominantly oral tradition of thought, and if liberation theology is done in lives rather than libraries, then a reading list, or a summary of particular theologians' works, is not the best introduction.

Within the confines of this medium of the printed word, I decided the most useful way in was through a glossary. Certain terms occur over and over again in the language of liberation theology: some are clear enough, but others have acquired almost a technical meaning.

By listing and explaining these recurrent terms, some of which have already occurred over and over again in the body of this book, I hope to give something of the flavour of liberation theology concerns, in the form of a simple key to decoding the language of those who speak it. The glossary should help to clarify and expand on some of the terms used in the book, and to elucidate the conceptual background into which they fit. It can also stand on its own, as a mini-introduction to the principal ideas of liberation theology.

But if you want really to get into the minds of those who do liberation theology, you must go and meet them — not just the theologians, but the poor who have found the Bible to contain words of life.

GLOSSARY

animator   Someone who leads a group, especially in the sense of offering inspiration and shape to a meeting. Rather than having generalized 'leaders' who could take on too much authority, leadership terms in the base communities tend to specify the kind of ministry a particular person is asked to exercise, as here to 'animate' a meeting. Whereas a **coordinator** would probably come from within the community, an animator might often be someone from outside the community who had more skills to offer. See also **catechist; ministries; pastoral agent**.

BEC   Basic ecclesial community, the English abbreviation corresponding to the Spanish or Portuguese **CEB**. Whereas CEB is pronounced 'seb', BEC is spelt out.

black theology   A term closely allied with liberation theology, associated especially with African and Afro-American theologians. See also *Damascus, The Road to*.

Boff, Leonardo   The most famous liberation theologian after Gustavo **Gutiérrez**. Boff is a Brazilian, who resigned from the Franciscans and from the priesthood in June 1992 in order to pursue his theology more freely. Among his works are *Church, Charism and Power* and *Ecclesiogenesis*.

CAL   The Pontifical Commission for Latin America (*Pontificia Commissio pro America Latina*), a Roman-appointed Commission with headquarters in the Vatican. To be distinguished from **CELAM**.

camino   (or, in Portuguese, *caminho* or *caminhada*) A very common concept of liberation theology for which it is practically impossible to find a standard equivalent in English. It is variously translated 'way', 'journey', 'pilgrimage', 'path' or 'progress'.

catechist   Someone who teaches the faith. Like **coordinator** or **animator**, this is another term for a base-community leader, though 'catechist' refers more to the fact that a person has a teaching role and is recognized by the local priest as having that ministry. Often, in the absence of a priest, a Sunday liturgy would be led by a catechist whose teaching role would be expressed in giving a sermon or leading a discussion. If there are several catechists within a community they might take turns. Catechists are responsible, e.g., for preparing children for first communion, parents for the baptism of their children, couples for marriage, and for helping the whole community to apply the scriptures to their lives. Catechists are often giving ongoing training through a series of short courses. See also **animator; coordinator; ministries; pastoral agent**.

CEB   *Comunidad* (Portuguese *comunidade*) *eclesial de base*, or basic ecclesial community. Pronounced 'seb', or in Portuguese 'sebee'.

CELAM   *Consejo* (Portuguese *Conselho*) *Episcopal Latinoamericano*, the Council of the Latin American Bishops, an elected body of delegates from all the Latin American and Caribbean countries. It meets regularly to coordinate the activities of the episcopate in the continent, and has its headquarters in Bogotá. The entire episcopate meets less frequently, at a General Conference of the Latin American Bishops, which has been held at Rio de Janeiro in 1955, at **Medellín** in 1968, at **Puebla** in 1979, and at **Santo Domingo** in 1992.

CNBB   *Conferência Nacional dos Bispos do Brasil*, the National Conference of Brazilian Bishops. Brazil is the only country in the world where a majority of the bishops were seen to be active supporters of liberation theology until the mid-1980s, although with more conservative appointments this can no longer be said.

The CNBB took a decisive step towards launching base communities in their Joint Pastoral Plan of 1965–70.

colonialism One of the major sins denounced by liberation theologians. Colonialism led the Western, developed nations, to dominate and exploit the third-world nations, originally through invading them and making them political colonies, but today more often through economic exploitation (this is sometimes called neo-colonialism). The effects of colonialism have been grave and lasting. 'One of the most serious and lasting legacies of European colonialism is racism' (*The Road to Damascus* 5). See also **cross and sword; imperialism; domination; exploitation**.

commitment The virtue of self-giving fidelity to the gospel, that gives people strength for the **struggle**. In Spanish it is *compromiso*, which however should be translated 'commitment' and not 'compromise'. See also **engagement; praxis**.

communism In many third-world countries, a term of extreme abuse used by the right wing against those who advocate social change. In many countries, to call someone a communist is to imply that that person deserves to die, and many death squads feel justified in murdering anyone who has been described as a communist. Any **struggle** for human rights, land reform or social justice can be taken as a legitimation for detecting 'communism'. One of Dom Hélder Câmara's famous remarks was 'When I give food to the poor they call me a saint; when I ask why the poor have no food they call me a communist'.

The Communist party as such does exist in many third-world countries, but this is very small compared to the broad range of people who are accused of being communist. Often there is an attempt by the left wing in third-world countries to dissociate itself from both communist and capitalist models, and to seek new solutions to the gross problems of poverty. This line of thought was expressed, for example, in a pastoral letter by the Nicaraguan bishops after the Sandinistas came to power in 1979 (though their optimism did not last): 'We are further confident that our revolutionary process will be something original, creative, truly Nicaraguan, and in no sense imitative. For what we, together with most

Nicaraguans, seek is a process that will result in a society completely and truly Nicaraguan, one that is neither capitalistic, nor dependent, nor totalitarian.'

conscientization or **consciousness-raising** Awareness-raising, particularly of the causes of social problems. A conscientized person is naturally led to take appropriate action in the light of his or her clearer understanding of the situation. 'Conscientization' is particularly associated with the educational methods of Paulo **Freire** (see Appendix 2).

contextual reading A way of reading the scriptures that takes into account the context of society today, and so enables the Bible to speak to current situations. Though base communities everywhere try to read the Bible contextually, the term is particularly associated with South Africa, where, for example, there is an Institute for Contextual Theology.

coordinator A leader of a group or base community, particularly when that leader comes from the people themselves. A coordinator 'coordinates' the different **ministries** operating in the community, so that the charisms of the Spirit can work harmoniously and effectively together. In practice this would include organizing meetings. Coordinator has slightly different connotations from **animator** although the terms are often interchangeable. See also **animator; catechist; pastoral agent**.

cross and sword In the process of colonization, the cross and the sword advanced together. 'The cross blessed the sword which was responsible for the shedding of our people's blood. The sword imposed the faith and protected the churches, sharing power and wealth with them' (*The Road to Damascus*, 3). Liberation theologians were keen that in the 1992 anniversary of Columbus' arrival in the West Indies, there should be no triumphalistic glorying in the arrival of Christianity in the Americas, without also a spirit of repentance for the way the cross was accompanied by the sword. See also **colonialism**.

culture See inculturation.

Damascus, The Road to Subtitled **Kairos and Conversion**, this is a theological proclamation from third-world Christians in countries where Christianity is misused to support oppressive governments. It was published in July 1989[4] and signed by

[4] Available from Catholic Institute for International Relations (CIIR), Unit 3, Canonbury Yard, 190a New North Road, Islington, London N1 7BJ; Center of Concern, 3700 13th Street NE, Washington, DC 20017; and Christian Aid, PO Box 100, London SE1 7RT.

a couple of thousand Christians (both Catholic and Protestant) from three continents and seven countries (El Salvador, Guatemala, Korea, Namibia, Nicaragua, the Philippines, South Africa). The document is of major importance for bringing together in a succinct and hard-hitting way a growing consensus of liberation theology around the world, which in different countries can be found under the following names: 'liberation theology, black theology, feminist theology, minjung theology, theology of struggle, the Church of the poor, the progressive Church, basic Christian communities' (Preamble).

The Conclusion explains: 'The particular crisis or kairos that has led us to the writing and signing of this proclamation of faith is the conflict between Christians in the world today. We have wished to make it quite clear that those Christians who side with the imperialists, the oppressors and the exploiters of people are siding with the idolaters who worship money, power, privilege and pleasure. To misuse Christianity to defend oppression is heretical. And to persecute Christians who are oppressed or who side with the oppressed is apostasy — the abandonment of the gospel of Jesus Christ.' See also *kairos*.

denunciation An aspect of the proclamation of the Gospel. We are simultaneously called to 'announce' the good news and to 'denounce' what is evil.

domination A sin denounced by liberation theologians. See also **colonialism**; **imperialism**; **exploitation**.

dream See **utopia**.

EATWOT The Ecumenical Association of Third World Theologians. Founded at Dar-es-Salaam in August 1976, the Association has provided a most important forum for the development of a united theological voice from the third world, with a characteristic freshness and incisiveness. In their own words, EATWOT 'strives to develop new models of theology that would interpret the Gospel in a more meaningful way to the peoples through: a deep rooting of the Christian message in their own culture; respectful dialogue with their traditions and popular religions; the praxis for integral liberation in relation to the situation of domination, poverty and oppression'. They publish a bi-annual theological journal called *Voices from the Third World*.

empower To enable marginalized people to take control of their lives, usually through helping them to organize. See **conscientization; organization; subjects**.

enable A term similar to **empower**, but more generalized.

engagement A commitment to some sort of gospel-inspired action or **praxis**. Someone is said to be 'engaged' when he or she is working on behalf of the poor in conditions that enable good theological thinking to emerge.

evangelical In Latin America, 'evangelical' tends to mean 'Protestant'.

evangelization by the poor A most important idea in liberation theology. Because the poor are in a special way the focus of the good news of Jesus, they have ears to hear the gospel message in a more acute and sensitive way than someone who is not poor. It is important, therefore, that the rest of the Church listens to the poor, to benefit from their insights into the gospel.

'Evangelization' is a word that is heard very much in the 1990s, because of the 'decade of evangelization' announced by John Paul II. There are different emphases to be found in the understanding of evangelization, from the simple proclamation of the gospel as a kind of ready-made package, to a more reciprocal process of dialogue and inculturation, in which respect is shown for the gospel values already present in a society, and the gospel is communicated as much by example as by words. See also **mission**.

exodus One of the most influential passages of scripture in liberation theology. The story of the Israelites' exodus from Egypt has been understood as bringing a promise of liberation from whatever enslaves a people, though the way to achieve that freedom is long and testing. The **Medellín** document, for example, said: 'Just as Israel of old, the first people (of God) felt the saving presence of God when God delivered them from the oppression of Egypt by the passage through the sea and led them to the promised land, so we also, the new people of God, cannot cease to feel God's saving passage in view of "true development, which is the passage for each and all, from conditions of life that are less human, to those that are more human." '[5]

exploitation Like **domination**, a term that frequently occurs in describing the forces of social sin.

[5] Introduction to the Final Documents, 6. The quote within the quote is from *Populorum Progressio*, 20.

feminist theology   Increasingly recognized as allied to, or even a branch of, liberation theology. In 1985, for example, **EAT-WOT** sponsored a conference of 28 women theologians from nine countries of the Caribbean and Latin America. North American and European feminists also regularly ally themselves with the theology of liberation. There can, however, be some differences of emphasis, particularly in the issue of women's ordination, which is not generally a concern of Latin American women, although the Letter from the Sixth Interecclesial Assembly of CEBs in Brazil appealed 'to the various forums of the Church, that they begin without delay the debate about the participation of women in the various levels of service, ministry and representation in the Church'. See also *Damascus, The Road to*.

Freire, Paulo   Brazilian educator with an enormous influence on base communities and liberation theology. See Appendix 2.

Gutiérrez, Gustavo   Known as 'the father of liberation theology', a Peruvian Indian theologian, who wrote a substantial book called *A Theology of Liberation*. The publication of this book in 1971 is often regarded as the decisive event which established liberation theology as a distinct theological school.

herald, Church as   A model for the Church. The Church is not so much a place of safety — a fortress or a holy city — as a herald to announce the dangerous, liberating news of Jesus Christ. The task of Christians is consequently to announce this good news, which will also involve denouncing the sins that stand in the way of liberation.

history   A key term in liberation theology. God is not a static being, dwelling in metaphysical aloofness, but a God who is involved in history, siding with the poor. 'Historical moment' is a term that often comes up, meaning that at different times and in different places, different forms of **praxis** are called for; we have to judge the demands of our own historical moment and respond accordingly. See also *kairos*.

idolatry   One of the grave sins, the 'sin of worshipping or being subservient to someone or something which is not God . . . In the Old Testament Moses and the prophets condemned the worship of the golden calf, the Baals and other idols made by human hands. In New Testament times the principal form of idolatry was the worship of mammon. The same is true for us today. In our countries, the worship of money, power, privilege and pleasure has certainly replaced the worship of God. This form of idolatry has been enthroned as a god.

Idolatry makes things, especially money and property, more important than people. It is anti-people' (*The Road to Damascus*, 49–50).

imperialism Closely allied to **colonialism**, imperialism is one of the grave sins, which has been responsible for the death of millions. 'Today most Third World countries', says *The Road to Damascus*, 'are no longer colonies, but we are still dominated by one or more imperial powers—the United States, Japan and Western Europe. Their web of economic control includes an unfair international trade system, multinational companies that monopolise strategic sections of our economy, economic policies dictated by lending banks and governments together with the International Monetary Fund and the World Bank. . . . The staggering size of Third World debt is only one dramatic sign of our subordination to imperialism. . . .'

The document continues: 'The effects of imperialism upon the Third World form a litany of woes: our children die of malnutrition and disease, there are no jobs for those who want to work, families break up to pursue employment abroad, peasants and indigenous communities are displaced from their land, most urban dwellers have to live in insanitary slums, many women have to sell their bodies, too many die without having lived a life that human persons deserve. We also suffer because of the plunder of our natural resources, and then we ourselves are being blamed for it' (9,12).

inculturation The process of expressing the Christian faith through the culture of a particular people. In the first two millennia, Christianity has developed through the thought-forms, art-forms, worship-forms and social customs of European culture, to the extent that Hilaire Belloc could say 'The faith is Europe, and Europe is the faith'. European inculturation, however, is only one possibility: if the gospel message is to be more widely heard in other cultures, new forms of inculturation will need to be accepted. To insist on a European inculturation of Christianity is a form of **imperialism**. Sometimes liberation theologians talk of 'incarnation' in this sense, stressing that God became flesh in a particular historical reality and culture: therefore the Church should continue to follow Christ's example by fully taking on the flesh of new historical realities and cultures. See Appendix 2 for Freire's ideas on culture.

individualism A prevalent sin—the sin of thinking only of oneself and one's immediate family, rather than accepting responsibility towards the community. Individualism leads to social injustice as each person struggles only for their own economic well-being, whereas community-awareness leads to a fairer distribution of resources, and a more powerful voice for the poor as they become organized. Whereas exploitation and domination are sins of the oppressors, individualism can also be a sin of the oppressed, by which they resist the social responsibilities that could lead to liberation. Oppressors will tend to encourage individualist tendencies among the poor, to avoid coordinated action and so keep them in their place.

Individualism can be seen in another way in traditions of spirituality that focus on 'me and God', overlooking my place in the community. This kind of individualistic interpretation of religion customarily goes with 'spiritualized' interpretations of the scriptures. See **spirituality**.

insertion   Placing oneself physically among the poor. Through being inserted one participates concretely in the life of a particular people or community and establishes an organic knot with them, coming to know their needs and outlook on life, and so, says Clodovis Boff in *Como Trabalhar com o Povo*,[6] insertion is the preliminary, indispensible condition for any kind of work with the people. There are many levels at which one may be inserted—meeting the members of a poor community occasionally or regularly, staying with them from time to time, working with them daily, or living among them. When bishops move from their palaces to live in poor areas (as some have done in Brazil) or when Sisters go to take a small house among the people instead of living in a large, isolated convent (as they are doing in many countries) this is for the sake of insertion among the people.

institutionalized violence   The situation of oppression in which thousands die from needless poverty and where any attempt to work for change is forcefully resisted, so that the people suffer violence at the hands of the institution. **Medellín** said that many parts of Latin America lived in such a 'situation of injustice that it can be called institutionalized violence'.[7] Paulo Freire wrote that 'With the establishment of a relationship of oppression, violence had *already* begun. Never in history has violence been initiated by the oppressed. How

[6] Chapter 4, p. 31.
[7] Document on *Peace*, 16.

could they be the initiators, if they themselves are the product of violence? . . . There would be no oppressed had there been no prior situation of violence to establish their subjugation.'[8]

Instruction on Certain Aspects of the Theology of Liberation   A Vatican document issued in 1984 by the Congregation for the Doctrine of the Faith, that showed great suspicion of liberation theology, on the grounds that it could fall into grave dangers and errors, particularly if Marxist ideas were uncritically accepted. It was followed in 1986 by a second instruction, the *Instruction on Christian Freedom and Liberation*, which aimed to present a more positive picture: this based its thinking more on European ideas than on Latin American ones.

jubilee year   The Old Testament tradition, whereby every fifty years outstanding debts would be cancelled, slaves released, and land restored. The idea of the jubilee gives theological backing to the call for remission of third-world debt today— not just as a matter of compassion, but as the mark of a just society, in which those who have unavoidably fallen into penury should eventually have a chance to remake their lives. See also **Luke 4**.

justice   A key concept in caring for those in need. Among those who give aid to the poor, the move from the concept of charity to that of justice has been an important transition in understanding. But this is not so much a new teaching as the recovery of an ancient one, as Pope Paul VI pointed out in his encyclical, ***Populorum Progressio***: 'Everyone knows that the fathers of the Church laid down the duty of the rich towards the poor in no uncertain terms. As St Ambrose put it: "You are not making a gift of what is yours to the poor man, but you are giving him back what is his. You have been appropriating things that are meant to be for the common use of everyone. The earth belongs to everyone, not to the rich." These words indicate that the right to private property is not absolute and unconditional. No one may appropriate surplus goods solely for his own private use when others lack the bare necessities of life' (23).

The struggle for justice is now widely accepted as an inescapable gospel imperative, not an afterthought. In 1971 the Synod of Bishops declared in their document, *Justice in the World*: 'Action on behalf of justice and participation in

---

[8] *Pedagogy of the Oppressed*, Pelican edition, p. 31.

the transformation of the world fully appear to us as a constitutive dimension of the preaching of the gospel' (6). See also **justice and peace**.

justice and peace Two concepts regularly linked to form a familiar phrase. Pope Paul VI inaugurated the Vatican's Justice and Peace Commission in 1967, 'to fulfil the wishes of the Council and to demonstrate the Holy See's concern for the developing nations'.[9] On its heels, national justice and peace commissions were set up by episcopal conferences, and numerous small justice and peace groups have sprung up at parish or deanery level all over the world. More recently, as a result of an initiative of the World Council of Churches, the environmental issue is sometimes added to the other two — 'justice, peace and integrity of creation'.

kairos A Greek word meaning 'moment'. The *kairos* in New Testament theology is a decisive point of special crisis and grace, for example, 'My *kairos* is at hand; I will keep the passover at your house with my disciples' (Matthew 26:18); 'You know how to interpret the appearance of earth and sky; but why do you not know how to interpret the present *kairos*?' (Luke 12:56).

The term became current in liberation thinking after the publication of an influential South African theological proclamation in 1985 called the *Kairos Document*, which said that 'the Kairos — the moment of truth — has arrived not only for apartheid, but also for the Church'. It uncompromisingly rejected the state's use of religion to defend injustice, criticized the Church for demanding 'reconciliation' between oppressors and oppressed, and challenged Christians 'to participate in the struggle for liberation and for a just society'. The *Road to Damascus* document drew inspiration from the *Kairos Document*, particularly when it said: 'We are faced with a *kairos*, a moment of truth, a time for decision, a time of grace, a God-given opportunity for conversion and hope' (43). See also **reconciliation, theology of; struggle**.

Letter to the Brazilian Bishops A document that has been much quoted to offset the negative impressions of the earlier *Instruction on Certain Aspects of the Theology of Liberation*. Dated 9 April 1986, the Letter was read to the Brazilian Episcopal Conference (CNBB) by Cardinal Gantin, and was immediately greeted with great joy in the hope that Rome had

[9] *Populorum Progressio*, 5.

changed its attitude to liberation theology. The famous quote says that 'the theology of liberation is not only opportune but useful and necessary'.

liberation The salvation announced by Jesus Christ, which is restricted neither to the afterlife nor to this world, but which embraces all that enslaves and imprisons human beings. Although the fullness of salvation can only be experienced in the next world, we are called to work towards it here on earth and to begin to live in the freedom of the children of God. Because of the highly spiritualized interpretation of 'salvation' that had become predominant, the theology of 'liberation' was seen as controversial for restoring more concrete elements—elements, for example, such as liberation from hunger and disease that play an important part in scripture. But it has never been true, as is sometimes said by critics, that the theology of liberation is concerned only with this-worldly interpretations of the gospel message. **Puebla** spoke of the 'integral liberation' of human beings as embracing 'both their earthly and transcendent dimensions'.[10]

Liberator A term frequently used as a standard title in the form 'Jesus Christ, Liberator', equivalent to 'Our Saviour Christ our Lord' in first-world theology. 'Liberator' after all means 'Saviour'. One of Leonardo Boff's books is also titled *Jesus Christ Liberator*.

Luke 4 A key text in liberation theology. Verses 16–21 give a clear and programmatic presentation of the gospel's preferential **option for the poor**. The text recounts how Jesus went to the synagogue at Nazareth and read a passage from Isaiah that described the ministry he had come to exercise — to preach the good news to the poor, to proclaim liberation for those imprisoned or oppressed and recovery of sight for the blind, and to announce the jubilee year of the Lord. See also **jubilee**.

Magnificat Another favourite passage in liberation theology. Mary's psalm of praise when she visits her cousin Elizabeth (Luke 1: 46–55) announces that God puts down the mighty from their thrones and exalts the downtrodden, fills the hungry with good things and sends the rich away empty. See also **Mary**.

marginalization The process of pushing people to the edge of society. The marginalized may live literally on the outskirts

---

[10] Document on *Evangelization, Liberation and Human Promotion*, 4.2 (475).

of cities in shanty-towns, or may be ignored for some other reason such as their colour, race, disabilities, creed, culture or language. See also **oppression; option for the poor.**

martyrdom A way of finding meaning in the brutal slaughter of so many today who work on behalf of the poor. Very many of those who have died in Latin America are regarded as martyrs, because they risked their lives from true Christian commitment and were killed for their commitment to Gospel ideals. Many of the best-known are clergy or religious or foreigners (the most famous is Monsignor Oscar **Romero** of El Salvador; but Chico Mendes, the Brazilian ecologist, is an exception to this rule), but there are thousands of others — mostly poor peasants, working away in the base communities on issues like land reform or human rights. Again and again Latin Americans have found that the sacrifice of the martyrs strengthens the faith of others, and they sometimes recall the words of Tertullian — 'the blood of Christians is the seed [of the Church]'.

Mary A much revered figure for the base communities. Jesus' mother is seen less as queen of heaven, and more as a model and example for the struggling oppressed, because she was a poor carpenter's wife, who gave birth in a stable in great poverty, who had to flee as a refugee to Egypt, and who saw her son tortured and killed. Above all she is seen as Mary of the **Magnificat.**

Medellín The second and most momentous General Conference of the Latin American and Caribbean bishops, held at Medellín, in Colombia, in 1968. It has been described by Enrique Dussel as 'the Vatican II of Latin America', and Gustavo **Gutiérrez** points to 1968 as the birthdate of Latin American liberation theology.[11] The meeting brought together the bishops of the continent at a decisive moment, when ideas were beginning to burgeon in the burst of creativity stimulated by Vatican II. Suddenly these initiatives were generally shared and obtained hierarchical approval and encouragement in the Medellín document.

The preferential **option for the poor** was affirmed: the mission of Christ 'centred on advising the poor of their liberation and he founded his Church as the sign of that poverty'.[12] The document called for 'a total change of Latin American

---

[11] *National Catholic Reporter* (11 December 1982), p. 11.
[12] Document on *The Poverty of the Church,* 7.

structures',[13] and pressed for 'a new order of justice that incorporates all persons in the decision-making of their own communities'.[14]

Base communities—which by this date were barely getting off the ground in a few advanced areas—received a tremendous boost of recognition and encouragement: see Appendix 3. See also **CELAM; Puebla; Santo Domingo; Vatican II.**

ministries Tasks or roles that people are called to exercise, on behalf of the community, in the service of God, whether ordained ministries (as deacon, priest or bishop) or not. In the base communities, everyone has a ministry of some sort, according to their charisms, or gifts of the Spirit. Lay ministries are not only leadership roles like **animator, coordinator, catechist**, but also include visiting the sick, looking after children, playing music, constructing buildings, giving legal advice, or any other task that can be performed for the benefit of the community, in the service of God.

minjung theology A Protestant theological movement from Korea, allied to the theology of liberation. *Min* means 'people' and *jung* means 'masses'. See also *Damascus, The Road to*.

mission Understood nowadays not only as proclamation of the gospel, but also as including **inculturation**, dialogue, and a preferential **option for the poor**. The missionary dimension is essential for any Christian community, no matter how small it is, if it is to be faithful to its calling as a cell of the Church.

mortal sin Once thought of as rather an outdated term, now recovered by liberation theology as a way of drawing attention to the gravity of sins that actually cause people to die. Archbishop **Romero** said 'We know that sin is truly "mortal"—not only because of the interior death of the one committing it, but because of the real, objective death it produces. And this reminds us of a profound datum of our Christian faith: sin is what put God's Son to death, and sin continues to be what puts God's sons and daughters to death.'[15]

new society A term often used of the vision of society for which we are working, as in 'The CEBs are a rehearsal of the Reign,

---

[13] Document on *Justice*, 16.
[14] *Message to the Peoples of Latin America.*
[15] Louvain, 2 February 1980.

the heart of the New Society, a little piece of God's Promised Land'.[16] See also **reign of God; utopia**.

oppression Frequently linked with **marginalization** and poverty. The oppressed, along with the poor and the marginalized, are spoken of as the special focus of the Church's concern. See also preferential **option for the poor**.

option for the poor An absolutely basic idea in liberation theology, based on the example of Jesus himself, of whom **Puebla** said 'the evangelization of the poor is the supreme sign and proof of his mission (Luke 7: 21–23)'.[17] The Vatican's customary phrase for the same idea is 'a love of preference for the poor', and some Anglicans speak of 'bias to the poor'.[18] The preferential option for the poor means quite simply that the gospel calls us to put the poor first. And so, when other factors are equal and a choice has to be made of where to concentrate resources, the Church chooses to give priority to the poor. Some critics have argued that because the word 'option' is used, therefore the preferential option for the poor is optional: but in fact 'option' here means 'choice'.

An option for the poor is taken when, for example, a religious congregation decides to stop running a fee-paying school to educate the children of the rich, and sends its sisters to work alongside the poor in an area of deprivation. An option for the poor is taken when a layperson qualified as, say, a doctor, chooses to settle in an inner-city slum rather than in a well-to-do suburb. An option for the poor is taken when a bishop invites the staff of a seminary to work with catechists from poor areas, so that training courses take a new shape under their influence.

There is not always agreement on who counts as 'poor': some say that we are all poor, because if we are not materially poor we are quite likely to be spiritually poor, or to have other problems that make us suffer apart from economic ones. But liberation theologians insist that the option for the poor should not be watered down so that it becomes meaningless: 'the poor' means the materially poor. See also **Medellín; Puebla**.

---

[16] Paragraph 9 of the final Letter from the Sixth Interecclesial Assembly of Basic Ecclesial Communities of Brazil, held at Trindade, Goiania, Brazil, 21–25 July 1986.

[17] Document on *A Preferential Option for the Poor*, 1.2, (1142).

[18] As in David Sheppard's book of that title.

organization The process by which a people organize themselves and become thereby empowered to affect their situation through common action. See also **empower**; **participation**.

orthopraxis 'Right praxis', seen as a condition for sound theology, restoring the balance from an older approach that would place exclusive stress on orthodoxy ('right teaching'). The idea is that our perceptions are very dependent on our angle of vision; theology done from an armchair is likely to be rather blind, considering that the central thrust of the gospel is to leave our armchair behind and become engaged. Orthodoxy and orthopraxis are complementary, rather than rival, conditions of good theology. See also **engagement**; **praxis**.

participation A key value, whether it is laity participating in their basic Christian community, or workers participating in decisions at their place of work, or a nation participating in the election of their government. Community is built when everyone plays a part.

pastoral agent A general term for any person who 'acts pastorally', especially where 'acting' is understood as being a leaven in a community — not to do things for the community, but to enable the community's own action to arise. Base communities do not arise spontaneously without someone acting as a pastoral agent, that is, taking an initiative that gets things going. Pastoral agents can be of two sorts: an external pastoral agent would be a sister or priest or layperson who comes into a community from outside to help facilitate the community in their own process; or an internal pastoral agent is someone who is already a member of the local people and of their class, but who has leadership gifts that stimulate the others. Anyone who is described as an **animator**, or **coordinator**, or **catechist**, would come under the broad heading of pastoral agent, as would all priests and religious.

pastoral circle or **pastoral cycle** Also known as the hermeneutical circle, and usually expressed as the sequence 'experience, social analysis, theological reflection, action'. It is seen as fundamentally similar to the 'see, judge, act' cycle that came out of Catholic Action, to which the Latin American Church often adds 'evaluate, celebrate'. It is a standard method of work for base communities.

pastoral planning A term that crops up in connection with coordinating priorities between communities, or parishes, or dioceses. In areas where base communities are encouraged, a high value is placed on pastoral planning, which enables representatives of the different communities to meet together with their pastors and form common strategies and campaigns, whether at the level of parish, deanery, diocese, or episcopal conference.

people   A word with special significance in liberation theology. In Spanish (and Portuguese) there are two words for 'people' — *gente* (Portuguese also *gente*) and *pueblo* (Portuguese *povo*). Whereas *la gente* means 'people' in a diverse and loose sense, *el pueblo* refers in a stronger way to '*a* people' more as a cultural unity: it can refer at one end of the scale to a particular village community, or at the other end to the great majority of the poor — conceived of not just as 'people' but as 'a people'. 'The chosen people', for example, uses the word *pueblo*, as does 'the people of God'. When liberation theologians talk repeatedly about 'the people', they are using the word *pueblo*, and usually implying a value assumption about the rights and needs of the poor majority.

poor, Church of the   See popular Church.

poor, preferential option for the   See option for the poor.

popular Church   A term meaning the Church of the people, which used to be associated with base communities in some Latin American countries. But since Pope John Paul II condemned the 'popular Church' in a visit to Nicaragua in 1983, the term has been rejected in favour of the 'Church of the poor'. **Puebla** commented: 'the appellation [popular Church] seems to be quite unfortunate. The popular Church seems to be something distinct from some "other" Church — the latter being identified with the "official" or "institutional" Church and accused of being "alienating". This suggests a division within the bosom of the Church and seems to imply an unacceptable denial of the hierarchy's function.'[19]

Populorum Progressio   An encyclical letter by Pope Paul VI, written in 1967, on issues of development, which took particular account of the injustice of poverty in the world today. One of its most famous quotations is 'development is the new name for peace'. See also **exodus; justice; justice and peace; social teaching of the Church**.

praxis   Close in meaning to 'practice', but with a stronger sense. Although we tend to think of praxis along the lines of action,

[19] Document on *The Truth about the Church: The People of God, Sign and Service of Communion*, 2.2, (263).

according to Paulo **Freire** authentic praxis has to include both action and reflection. Theology that does not emerge out of action will be a useless, abstract, word game and will not come to grips with the essential teaching of Jesus. The critique of European theology is this lack of a basis in practice. The theology of liberation leads into practice, and also emerges out of practice. Theologians should themselves have some form of a praxis, and not just recommend action to others. See also **engagement** and Appendix 2.

preferential option for the poor   See option for the poor.

project   A goal for society towards which the Christian community is working. In liberation theology, the word *proyecto* has a stronger meaning than is usually associated with the English 'project'.

Puebla   The next General Conference of the Latin American and Caribbean bishops after **Medellín**, in Puebla, Mexico, in January 1979. Although there was more tension at this meeting between those favouring liberation theology and those opposed, the final documents nonetheless included some worthwhile advances, so that Medellín and Puebla are often cited as authorities, and mentioned in the same breath as each other, and as **Vatican II**: 'the latter two episcopal conferences and their documents contribute to Vatican II by concretizing, extending and projecting its insights'.[20]

On the option for the poor, Puebla gave a ringing endorsement of what was said at Medellín. On base communities, Puebla was now using the term **CEBs** where Medellín had used the earlier formulation, 'basic Christian communities'. See also **CELAM; Santo Domingo**.

reality   A favourite term of liberation theologians, though *realidad* (*realidade* in Portuguese) is rarely translated 'reality'. It means the actual situation, things as they currently are, the world we live in. The 'reality' of one place will be different from that of another, and theologians should make their first task to see, understand, and then respond to the 'reality' wherever they are, which might encompass elements like, for example, a housing shortage, inflation, the influence of a multi-national company with a local factory, gang violence, child abuse, a drought, etc. Without a grounding in the real world, theology becomes unreal.

[20] Marcello Azevedo, *Basic Ecclesial Communities in Brazil*, p. 51.

reconciliation, theology of Generally understood as opposed to liberation theology. A theology of reconciliation wants to avoid the unpleasantness of conflict, and tends to urge peace at the expense of justice. It usually amounts to supporting the *status quo*. For example, a theology of reconciliation in a South African situation would urge the black population to avoid making strident and disturbing demands. Needless to say, liberation theologians are in favour of true reconciliation, but believe this can sometimes be attained only through pain and struggle.

reformism Used in a disparaging way by liberation theologians, because to reform a system implies that the underlying structure is to be maintained, whereas in the situations they are generally dealing with in Latin America, the system is so thoroughly evil that a complete change — a revolution — is required.

reign of God Another term for the kingdom of God, though in Spanish (and Portuguese) there is only the one word, *reino*. The reign of God is one in which justice and peace prevail and no one is hungry, oppressed or in need. The mission of Christians is to work towards making the world more the kind of place in which God rules and God's will is done. The reign, therefore, is both gift and task. The reign is both now and to come: it is an ideal that is never achieved in this world but is always ahead of us, and yet the demands of the reign already direct us towards the transformation of society. See also **new society; utopia**.

revolution A fundamental change of the system, whether achieved through violent or peaceful means. **Reformism** by contrast wants to maintain essentially the same system, while making minor adjustments in it.

Road to Damascus See *Damascus, The Road to*.

Romero, Oscar Former Archbishop of El Salvador, and the most famous and revered of all Latin American martyrs. He upheld the cause of the poor and appealed against government repression. He was shot while saying mass on 24 March 1980.

Santa Fe document A couple of reports prepared for the US government in the early 1980s which warned that basic Christian communities and liberation theology were a danger to US political interests. The recent explosion of politically conservative, fundamentalist sects in Latin America is widely believed to be largely due to funding from US sources, in an attempt to control the spread of liberation theology. It is not known whether or to what extent the same sources may also have stimulated attempts to curb liberation theology from within the Catholic Church.

Santo Domingo The fourth General Conference of the Latin American and Caribbean Bishops in 1992, in the Dominican Republic — the first place where Columbus landed in 1492. The meeting was held amidst tensions, as many felt that the Vatican had taken over the agenda from the competence of the local bishops, ignored the extensive preparatory work that had been done, and imposed a final document that was not a genuine product of the conference. Optimists however could detect an advance in what the document said about different cultures (see **inculturation**).

There were also tensions over the need to ask forgiveness for the crimes committed against the indigenous peoples of the continent as a result of the European invasion 500 years earlier. The more Roman-minded delegates feared that the confidence to evangelize (in the decade of evangelization, the 1990s) would be shaken by revealing a penitent approach concerning the first arrival of the gospel from Europe. See also **CELAM; Medellín; Puebla.**

social teaching of the Church The official teaching of the magisterium on social issues. It is sometimes said to be 'the Church's best kept secret' because there is such widespread ignorance of it and so few serious attempts to implement it. Though inevitably the Church's social teaching has a rather European flavour and is articulated in a different way from liberation theology, it is still welcomed as an ally, for defending human rights, upholding the rights of workers, insisting on the responsibilities of the rich nations to establish fairer trading relations, etc. Though its source is in scripture and early tradition, the social teaching of the Church is generally dated from an encyclical by Pope Leo XIII in 1891 called *Rerum Novarum*, which was regarded as shockingly socialist by many at the time. The most celebrated modern documents are Pope John XXIII's *Pacem in Terris* (1963) and Pope Paul VI's *Populorum Progressio*. Pope John Paul II has issued two encyclicals on the Church's social teaching — *Laborem Exercens* (1981) and *Sollicitudo Rei Socialis* (1988).[21]

[21]Texts can be found in *Proclaiming Justice and Peace*, ed. Walsh and Davies (see Bibliography).

solidarity   A value in the people's struggle. Through solidarity a people becomes strong and can achieve its objectives, rather than being picked off one by one as individuals.

spirituality   Always present in liberation theology, though with a different emphasis from European spirituality. At one time spirituality seemed to have earned rather a bad reputation, as 'spiritualized' interpretations of the scriptures would attempt to eliminate any concrete or material meaning, in order to focus exclusively on inner attitudes. For example, Matthew's version of the beatitude, 'Blessed are the poor in spirit', would always be quoted in preference to Luke's 'Blessed are you poor'. Although such spiritualized interpretation is still the prevalent tendency in first-world theology, liberation theology has begun to devote more conscious attention to spirituality, trying to purify the term from passivist connotations. Virtues like truth, love of the poor, justice and giving one's life for others are true spirituality, they say.

struggle   In Spanish, *lucha*, in Portuguese, *luta*. The struggle is a key term for the experiences that Christians must expect as they proclaim the good news of Jesus and work towards building the reign of God. In the Philippines, the term 'theology of struggle' is used more than 'liberation theology'.

subjects   Those who know and act for themselves, as opposed to those who are merely the objects of others' knowledge and action. The poor are called, not just to suffer passively what is done to them, but actively to effect change. When charity is administered to the poor, the people remain objects. But when **pastoral agents** work *with* the poor, **empowering** them, they enable the poor to take history into their own bands and act for themselves. See also **conscientization**.

subversive memory of Jesus Christ   A phrase used to remind us that 'subversive' is a criticism levelled not just against the followers of liberation theology, but against Jesus himself. Leonardo Boff, for example, speaks of 'the liberative dimensions of faith — the so-called "perilous, subversive memory of Jesus Christ" who was crucified by the powers of this world and raised up by God to demonstrate the divine and human triumph of a life sacrificed for the cause of the total liberation of human beings, especially of the impoverished.'[22]

theologian   An important ministry in the service of the poor. A good theologian is not a mere academic shut up in a

[22]*Ecclesiogenesis*, p. 38.

scholarly institute, but a theologian of the **people**, gifted with a charism or entrusted with a ministry for the benefit of the community. It has been said by some that the theologian's task is no more than to articulate what the people say about God: after all, it is the poor who are in a position to hear the good news in an especially vivid way. But there is certainly need of those with a knowledge of scripture and Christian tradition, as well as a gift for articulation and analysis, who can shine the light of Gospel clarity into real situations. See also **evangelization by the poor**; **praxis**.

utopia The future society of Justice and peace towards which Christians are working, and which always lies ahead as an inspiring ideal. The utopia, or dream, or vision, is what inspires us in the **struggle**.

Vatican II The inspiration and indirect authority for modern liberation theology, largely because of the Council's emphasis on discerning the signs of the times. Liberation theologians see their work as an authentic continuation of the spirit of the Second Vatican Council—which for Latin America was particularly complemented by the **Medellín** meeting of **CELAM**. The Conciliar document *Gaudium et Spes* is seen as of special importance, with its famous opening words which tie the Church so intimately into the struggles of the world today: 'The joys and the hopes, the griefs and the anxieties of the people of this age, especially those who are poor or in any way afflicted, these too are the joys and hopes, the griefs and anxieties of the followers of Christ.'

2

An Introduction to Paulo Freire

It is widely accepted that Paulo Freire, the Brazilian educator of the poor, has had an extensive influence on the methods of the basic Christian communities. This Appendix gives a brief introduction to Freire's thought, principally through the ideas of his most famous book, *Pedagogy of the Oppressed*.

Freire was born in 1921 in Recife, Brazil, to a middle-class family, but knew great poverty as a child because of the depression. He found himself falling behind at school, because of listlessness due to hunger. At the age of eleven he made a vow to dedicate himself to the struggle against hunger.

In due course Freire became Professor of the History and Philosophy of Education in the University of Recife, and from there he coordinated the Adult Education Programme of the Popular Culture Movement. Around this time there were about 80,000 children in Recife not in school, and the proportion of adult illiteracy was estimated at 60 to 70 per cent. Whereas other crusades against illiteracy had met with little success, Freire believed adults could learn to read rapidly if it were not presented as a cultural imposition, but began with their own situation. It was found that his materials would teach adults to read in 30 to 40 hours, and his methods became widely used by Catholics and others in literacy campaigns throughout the north-east of the country.

Unfortunately the upper and middle classes in Brazil became increasingly frightened of the growing political awareness of the people, and there was a military coup in 1964. It is estimated that 20,000 literacy circles would have been functioning in Brazil in 1964 if the military had not ended the programme.

Freire himself was first put under house arrest, then imprisoned for 70 days, and finally had to flee the country. He went to Chile where he worked for five years with UNESCO, then acted as consultant at Harvard University's School of Education, and in 1970 went to work for the World Council of Churches in Geneva.

PRACTICAL METHOD

Freire developed a method of using ten picture cards, very primitive in their style of art. The process of discussing the pictures was called 'conscientization', because it encouraged people to analyse their reality, become more aware of the constraints on their lives, and take action to transform the situation. (Many people say Freire invented the term 'conscientization', or rather—in Portuguese—*conscientização*. He denies this,[1] but he was probably the first person to put it into print.)

The pictures illustrated the distinction between nature and culture. The first one showed a man with a well, a tree, a house, a hoe and a pig. Freire would ask questions like 'Who made the well?' and 'Who made the tree?', to elicit the awareness that people use natural materials to change their situation and create culture.

[1] 'The word was born during a series of round table meetings of professors at the Brazilian Institute of Higher Studies (ISEB), which was created after the "liberating" revolution of 1964, under the wing of the Ministry of Education. The word was excogitated by some one of the professors there, but I really can't remember who. Anyway, it came out of our group reflections . . . As soon as I heard it, I realized the profundity of its meaning, since I was fully convinced that education, as an exercise in freedom, is an act of knowing, a critical approach to reality. It was inevitable, then, that the word became a part of the terminology I used thereafter to express my pedagogical views, and it easily came to be thought of as something I had created. Hélder Câmara was the one who popularized the term and gave it currency in English. Thus, thanks to him rather than to me, the word caught on in Europe and in the United States': 'Conscientizing as a Way of Liberating' in Hennelly (ed.), *Liberation Theology: A Documentary History*, pp. 5–6.

The discussion would give them the words to 'name' this distinction between nature and culture.

Another picture showed a man, wearing a feather headdress, shooting a bird with a bow and arrow. ('What is the difference between feathers on the bird and feathers on the headdress?') And another showed a man shooting a bird with a gun. (Here is a tool so complex that written instructions are needed for its manufacture.) Then there was a flower arrangement: in discussing this, one woman said 'I make culture. I know how to do that.' Another card showed someone making pots, and this drew the response from a peasant, 'I make shoes, and now I discover that I have as much value as a professor who makes books.'

Then a team, working with local volunteers, would spend a considerable period of time in the community, listening, and noticing the way people talk, their style of life, at work and at leisure. As a result of this investigation they would draw up a list of 'generative' words for that particular community, choosing words that were, on the one hand, familiar, everyday vocabulary, and, on the other, suitable for illustrating the range of syllabic sounds. For example, the list produced for a slum in Recife was as follows (but in, of course, their local Portuguese): brick, vote, crab, straw, odd job, ashes, illness, fountain, sewing machine, employment, sugar mill, swamp, land, hoe, class.

Then one word would be taken — say *tojolo*, which means 'brick' — and taught to the group, by using it as a caption on a picture of a construction scene. Next a 'card of discovery' was made as follows:

ta	te	ti	to	tu
ja	je	ji	jo	ju
la	le	li	lo	lu

From this Freire would encourage people to make new words, for example, *luta*, 'struggle'; or *loja*, 'store'.

There is a story that a visitor came to see how one of these 'circles of culture' operated, in Rio Grande do Norte. The group had been going some time, and a woman was able to read out a telegram from a newspaper about the exploitation of salt locally. The visitor asked 'Do you know what "exploitation" means?' The woman replied 'Perhaps you, a rich young man, don't know. But I, a poor woman, I know what exploitation is.'

PEDAGOGY OF THE OPPRESSED

Freire's best-known book is *Pedagogy of the Oppressed*, of which he says that 'Christians and Marxists, though they may disagree with me in part or in whole, will continue reading to the end'.[2] The term 'conscientization' (p. 15) is at the forefront of this book, as of all Freire's thought: it has become an everyday word in the world of liberation theology, even if it is something of a tongue-twister to pronounce.

Human beings, says Freire, are 'subjects' (p. 16), meaning that they can know and act, and not just be the object of others' knowing and acting. They have a 'vocation', which is 'humanization'. Humanization is constantly 'thwarted by injustice, exploitation, oppression, and the violence of the oppressors; it is affirmed by the yearning of the oppressed for freedom and justice, and by their struggle to recover their lost humanity' (p. 20).

Freire draws attention to the delusions of false charity from the oppressors: 'in order to have the continued opportunity to express their "generosity", the oppressors must perpetuate injustice as well. An unjust social order is the permanent fount of this "generosity" ' (p. 21). 'False charity constrains the fearful and subdued, the "rejects of life", to extend their trembling hands. Real generosity lies in striving so that those hands — whether of individuals or entire peoples — need be extended less and less in supplication, so that more and more they become human hands which work and, by working, transform the world' (p. 22).

Freire points out the tendency of the oppressed to take on the values of the oppressor. 'The oppressed must not, in seeking to regain their humanity . . . become in turn oppressors of the oppressors, but rather restorers of the humanity of both' (p. 21). Yet it is an ever-present pitfall, because the model of humanity they have been given is that of the oppressor. 'It is a rare peasant who, once "promoted" to overseer, does not become more of a tyrant towards his former comrades than the owner himself' (p. 23).

The oppressor becomes 'housed' within the oppressed, and the oppressed have a 'fear of freedom' because they have internalized the image of the oppressor. 'Freedom would require them to eject this image and replace it with autonomy and responsibility.

---

[2] *Pedagogy of the Oppressed*, Pelican edition, p. 17. Other page references in the text of this Appendix are to the same edition of this book.

Freedom is acquired by conquest, not by gift. It must be pursued constantly and responsibly' (pp. 23–4).

'Self-depreciation is another characteristic of the oppressed, which derives from their internalization of the opinion the oppressors hold of them' (p. 38). They tend to go along with the boss in saying 'What can I do? I'm only a peasant' (p. 37). Along with this lack of confidence goes 'a diffuse, magical belief in the invulnerability and power of the oppressor' (p. 39).

Liberation is not achieved without profound conflict and pain, for in the new situation the former oppressors genuinely consider themselves to be oppressed. 'Formerly, they could eat, dress, wear shoes, be educated, travel, and hear Beethoven; while millions did not eat, had no clothes or shoes, neither studied nor travelled, much less listened to Beethoven. Any restriction on this way of life, in the name of the rights of the community, appears to the former oppressors as a profound violation of their individual rights— although they had no respect for the millions who suffered and died of hunger, pain, sorrow, and despair. For the oppressors, "human beings" refers only to themselves; other people are "things" ' (p. 34).

For the oppressor, *'having more* is an inalienable right, a right they acquired through their own "effort", with their "courage to take risks". If others do not have more, it is because they are incompetent and lazy, and worst of all is their unjustifiable ingratitude towards the "generous gestures" of the dominant class' (p. 35).

Freire points out that if it wishes to stay in power, the oppressor class needs to avoid as potentially subversive anything that unites and organizes the people. 'Concepts such as unity, organization, and struggle, are immediately labelled as dangerous' (p. 111). In an attempt to avoid united, community action, they will rather aim 'to inoculate individuals with the bourgeois appetite for personal success' (p. 119).

Nonetheless, it is a fact that some members of the oppressor class join the oppressed in their struggle for liberation. But even then they have a tendency to distrust the people's ability, and tend to assume that they themselves must be the agents of the transformation. And so 'conversion to the people requires a profound rebirth' (p. 37).

One way in which the dominant class can stay uppermost is through the subtle tool of 'cultural invasion'. 'For cultural invasion to succeed, it is essential that those invaded become convinced of their intrinsic inferiority. Since everything has its opposite, if those who are invaded consider themselves inferior, they must necessarily recognize the superiority of the invaders. The values of the latter thereby become the pattern for the former. The more invasion is accentuated and those invaded are alienated from the spirit of their own culture and from themselves, the more the latter want to be like the invader: to walk like them, dress like them, talk like them' (p. 122). What is required by contrast is that those 'who come from "another world" to the world of the people do so not as invaders. They do not come to *teach* or to *transmit* or to *give* anything, but rather to learn, with the people, about the people's world' (p. 147).

It is crucial that any liberation must be forged '*with*, and not *for*, the oppressed' (p. 25). 'We cannot say that in the process of revolution someone liberates someone else, not yet that someone liberates himself, but rather that people in communion liberate each other. This affirmation is not meant to undervalue the importance of revolutionary leaders but, on the contrary, to emphasize their value. What could be more important than to live and work with the oppressed, with the "rejects of life", with the "wretched of the earth"? In this communion, the revolutionary leaders should find not only their *raison d'être* but a motive for rejoicing' (p. 103).

And so 'the oppressor shows solidarity with the oppressed only when he stops regarding the oppressed as an abstract category and sees them as persons who have been unjustly dealt with, deprived of their voice, cheated in the sale of their labour—when he stops making pious, sentimental, and individualistic gestures and risks an act of love. True solidarity is found only in the plenitude of this act of love, in its existentiality, in its praxis' (p. 26).

Praxis is another key word, and by it Freire means 'reflection and action upon the world in order to transform it' (p. 28). It is essential that praxis includes both elements of action and reflection. When one or the other is absent, it is no longer praxis. 'When a word is deprived of its dimension of action, reflection automatically suffers as well; and the word is changed into idle chatter, into *verbalism*, into an alienated and alienating "blah". . . . On the other hand, if action is emphasized exclusively, to the detriment of reflection, the word is converted into *activism*. The latter—action for action's sake —negates the true praxis and makes dialogue impossible' (p. 60).

Action and reflection do not however have to occur simultaneously. There is a valid place for 'the silence of profound meditation, in which people only apparently leave the world, withdrawing from it in order to consider it in its totality, and thus remaining with it. But this type of retreat is only authentic when the meditator is "bathed" in reality' (p. 61). It is rather that action and reflection feed into each other, just as we see in the idea of the pastoral circle.[3] 'Reflection—true reflection—leads to action. On the other hand, when the situation calls for action, that action will constitute an authentic praxis only if its consequences become the object of critical reflection' (p. 41).

True reflection cannot come through the traditional 'banking concept of education, in which the scope of action allowed to the students extends only as far as receiving, filing, and storing the deposits' (p. 46). 'Authentic liberation—the process of humanization—is not another "deposit" to be made in people. Liberation is a praxis: the action and reflection of people upon their world in order to transform it' (p. 52).

The oppressed must be convinced through their own reflection of the need for 'struggle' (another key word[4]). And so, rather than the banking concept, what is needed is 'problem-posing' education (p. 52) through the method of dialogue (p. 42). 'Through dialogue, the teacher-of-the-students and the students-of-the-teacher cease to exist . . . They become jointly responsible for a process in which all grow' (p. 53). Through dialogue, people 'name the world', and to name the world is 'to change it', because 'to speak a true word is to transform the world' (pp. 60–1).

Faith, hope and love are all involved: 'Faith in humanity is an *a priori* requirement for dialogue; the "dialogical person" believes in other people even before meeting them face to face' (p. 63). 'Nor yet can dialogue exist without hope. Hope is rooted in people's incompleteness, from which they move out in constant search' (p. 64). The dialogue and the struggle are acts of love. 'The naming of the world, which is an act of creation and re-creation, is not possible if it is not infused with love . . . No matter where the oppressed are found, the act of love is commitment to their cause—the cause of liberation' (p. 62).

FREIRE AS A CHRISTIAN THINKER

For those who have had no previous contact with third-world theology, Freire's ideas can sound alarmingly Marxist. His approach to gospel teaching is so radical that people can simply miss the deep

---

[3] See Appendix 1.
[4] See Appendix 1.

Christian roots of his thinking. In fact Freire sees his whole being as drenched in commitment to the gospel. For him, being a Christian and being a revolutionary (that is to say, working for a radical change of society and not just minor adjustments through reforms) were not only compatible positions, but they implied each other. 'Being a Christian, a revolutionary: these are very close.'[5] Both are ways of knowing our profound imperfections and committing ourselves to becoming more fully human: 'I am a Christian revolutionary or a revolutionary Christian because I know that I want to become.'[6]

Christian influence is very evident in Freire's idea of the need for 'rebirth'.

> *Conscientization demands an Easter. That is, it demands that we die to be reborn again. Christians must live their Easter, and that too is a utopia. Those who don't make their Easter, in the sense of dying in order to be reborn, are not real Christians. That is why Christianity is, for me, such a marvelous doctrine. People have accused me of being a communist, but no communist could say what I have just said. I have never had any temptation to cease being a Catholic. The reason is that I am not yet completely a Catholic; I just keep on trying to be one more completely, day after day. The condition of being is to go on being. I have never yet felt that I had to leave the Church, or set aside my Christian convictions, in order to say what I have to say, or go to jail—or even refuse to. I just feel passionately, corporately, physically, with all my being, that my stance is a Christian one because it is 100 per cent revolutionary and human and liberating, and hence committed and utopian. And that, as I see it, must be our position, the position of a Church that must not forget it is called by its origins to die shivering in the cold.*[7]

[5] Margaret Costigan, *You Have the Third World Inside You: An Interview with Paulo Freire* (Workers' Educational Association S.E. Scotland District, 1982).

[6] *Ibid.*

[7] From 'Conscientizar para Liberar', in the Mexican quarterly *Contacto* 8: 1 (1971) pp. 43–51, translated in Hennelly (ed.), *Liberation Theology: A Documentary History*, p. 13. Minor adjustments to translation have been made along the lines of the version in Daniel S. Schipani, *Conscientization and Creativity: Paulo Freire and Christian Education* (University Press of America, 1984). For **utopia** see Appendix 1.

Christian thinking is also clearly present in his reverence for 'the word', which transforms the world it comes into, and is the right of all who are in the world. Closely linked to this, Freire explains that his key idea of 'naming' came to him from Genesis 2. 'One of the things that excited me in the Bible was in Genesis when God said . . . to the human beings that they would give a name to the things. I read this when I was very young and I never forgot it.'[8]

We see a clearly Christian background, too, when he speaks of the retreat, as a period for the silence of profound meditation. Finally, his Christian evocation of the trio of virtues, faith, hope and love (p. 175), cannot go unnoticed.

Freire's Christian commitment does not mean that he is uncritical of the Church. In at least one period of his life he found the contradiction intolerable between the pious words said at Sunday services and the lack of everyday commitment. In a paper on education and the Church[9] he explicitly criticized both the colonialist, traditional Church and the reformist, modernizing Church. But at a deeper level he believes in the Church, as this passage on freedom and salvation shows:

> *Freedom isn't something that is given. It is*
> *something very arduous, because nobody gives*
> *freedom to anyone else, no one frees another,*
> *nobody can even free him or herself all alone;*
> *humans free themselves only in concert, in*
> *communion, collaborating on something wrong that*
> *they want to correct. There is an interesting*
> *theological parallel to this: no one saves another, no*
> *one saves him or herself all alone, because only in*
> *communion can we save ourselves — or not save*
> *ourselves. You don't save me, because my soul, my*
> *being, my conscious body is not something that A or*
> *B can save. We work out our salvation in*
> *communion.*[10]

[8] Costigan, *op. cit.*
[9] *Las Iglesias, la Educación y el proceso de Liberación Humana en la Historia* (La Aurora, Buenos Aires, 1974).
[10] In Hennelly, *op. cit.*, p. 12.

INFLUENCE ON BASE COMMUNITIES

Turning now more specifically to our theme of basic Christian communities, we end by enumerating the following ideas which have come in one way or another via the influence of Freire's thought:

- conscientization;
- justice rather than charity, the need to change the structures and not just alleviate the symptoms;
- giving a sense of dignity to the poor;
- liberation as also liberation of the rich, even if they resist it: rather than hatred between classes the aim is humanization for all;
- the need for the people to be organized;
- the importance of the people's own culture;
- working 'with and not for' the poor;
- the indivisibility of reflection and action, each needing to move on into the other, in a 'pastoral circle' sequence;
- the 'struggle' — a word which comes up again and again in liberation theology;
- the need for a considerable period of time inserted in a community, listening to their everyday concerns, before beginning to teach the people anything.

We have seen enough to understand why it has become so habitual to link the name of Freire with basic Christian communities. It is not just that Freire's work and basic ecclesial communities both began in Brazil around the same time. Nor is it a matter of a deliberate adherence to his ideas, as some kind of an authority: indeed many people who regularly quote the name Freire have never actually studied his work. Rather, there are elements in his legacy that have entered the oral tradition, and so played an enduring role in shaping the approach of base communities everywhere.

Documentation:

Key texts from the Conferences of Latin American Bishops and from the Vatican

MEDELLÍN

The General Conference of Latin American Bishops at Medellín[1] in 1968 heralds the launch, throughout the Latin American continent, of liberation theology and also of basic Christian communities, which are described as the 'initial cell' of Church structure. They are to be led in many cases by laity, preferably coming from the communities themselves, and these animators are to be encouraged in a spirit of independence and initiative.

This passage comes from the document *Pastoral de Conjunto*.

Basic Christian Communities

10. Christians ought to find their way of living out the communion to which they have been called in

---

[1] See Appendix 1

the 'base community', that is to say, in a community
of their locality or of their ambience which is a
homogeneous group and which has a size that allows
for personal, fraternal contact among its members.
Consequently, the Church's pastoral efforts must be
oriented toward the transformation of these
communities into a 'family of God', beginning by
making itself present among them as leaven by
means of a nucleus such that, even if it be small, it
creates a community of faith, hope and charity.[2]
Thus the Christian base community is the first and
fundamental ecclesial nucleus, which on its own level
must make itself responsible for the richness and
expansion of the faith, as well as of the cult which is
its expression. This community, then, is the initial
cell of the ecclesial structure and the focus of
evangelization, and at present it is a fundamental
factor in human promotion and development.

11. The essential element for the existence of
Christian base communities are their leaders or
organizers. These can be priests, deacons, religious
men or women, or laity. It is desirable that they
belong to the community which they animate. The
selection and formation of leaders ought to be a
matter of top priority in the concerns of parish
priests and bishops, who must always be mindful
that moral and spiritual maturity depends in large
measure on the assumption of responsibilities in a
climate of autonomy.[3]

The members of these communities, 'living in
accord with the vocation to which they have been
called, exercise the functions that God has entrusted
to them, priestly, prophetical and royal', and thus
make of their community 'a sign of the presence of
God in the world'.[4]

12. It is recommended that serious studies be made,
of a theological, sociological and historical nature,
concerning these Christian base communities, which

---

[2] Cf. Vatican Council II, Dogmatic Constitution *Lumen Gentium*, no. 8.
[3] Cf. Vatican Council II, Pastoral Constitution *Gaudium et Spes*, no. 55.
[4] Cf. Vatican Council II. Decree *Ad Gentes*, no. 15.

are beginning to burgeon today after having been a key point in the pastoral work of the missionaries who implanted the Faith and the Church in our continent. It is also recommended that the experiences which are going on be publicized through CELAM and that they be coordinated in so far as this is possible.

EVANGELII NUNTIANDI

Following the 1974 Synod of Bishops in Rome on the theme of evangelization in the modern world, Pope Paul VI issued in 1975 a document called *Evangelii Nuntiandi* (the first two words of the document in Latin — 'On proclaiming the Gospel'), which summed up the Synod's discussion. The treatment of base communities is quite detailed, and has served as a basis for subsequent Vatican statements on the subject. In summary, base communities are hailed as a 'hope for the universal Church' providing they remain truly ecclesial, that is united to the Church through the hierarchical structures. Probably the more anti-institutional, European 'base communities' have a great deal to do with this hesitancy, though of course we should not underestimate the radical challenge posed by all base communities to the habitual ways in which clerical authority is exercised.

The full text can be found in *Proclaiming Justice and Peace*, edited by Walsh and Davies.

Basic communities

58. *The last synod devoted considerable attention to these small communities, or base communities, because they are often talked about in the Church today. What are they, and why should they be the special beneficiaries of evangelization and at the same time evangelizers themselves?*

58.1 *According to the various statements heard in the synod, such communities flourish more or less throughout the Church. They differ greatly among* *themselves, both within the same region and even more so from one region to another.*

58.2 *In some regions they appear and develop, almost without exception, within the Church, having solidarity with her life, being nourished by her teaching and united with her pastors. In these cases, they spring from the need to live the Church's life more intensely, or from the desire and quest for a more human dimension such as larger ecclesial communities can only offer with difficulty, especially in the big modern cities which lend themselves both to life in the mass and to anonymity. Such communities can quite simply be in their own way an extension on the spiritual and religious level—worship, deepening of faith, fraternal charity, prayer, contact with pastors—of the small sociological community such as the village, etc. Or again their aim may be to bring together, for the purpose of listening to and meditating on the word, for the sacraments and the bond of the* agape, *groups of people who are linked by age, culture, civil state or social situation: married couples, young people, professional people, etc., people who already happen to be united in the struggle for justice, brotherly aid to the poor, human advancement. In still other cases they bring Christians together in places where the shortage of priests does not favour the normal life of a parish community. This is all presupposed within communities constituted by the Church, especially individual churches and parishes.*

58.3 *In other regions, on the other hand, base communities come together in a spirit of bitter criticism of the Church, which they are quick to stigmatize as 'institutional' and to which they set themselves up in opposition as charismatic communities, free from structures and inspired only by the gospel. Thus their obvious characteristic is an attitude of fault-finding and of rejection with regard to the Church's outward manifestations: her hierarchy, her signs. They are radically opposed to the Church. By following these lines their main inspiration very quickly becomes ideological, and it* *rarely happens that they do not quickly fall victim to some political option or current of thought, and then to a system, even a party, with all the attendant risks of becoming its instrument.*

58.4 *The difference is already notable: the communities which by their spirit of opposition cut themselves off from the Church, and whose unity they wound, can well be called base communities, but in this case it is a strictly sociological name. They could not, without a misuse of terms, be called basic ecclesial communities, even if, while being hostile to the hierarchy, they claim to remain within the unity of the Church. This name belongs to the other groups, those which come together within the Church in order to unite themselves to the Church and to cause the Church to grow.*

58.5 *These latter communities will be a place of evangelization, for the benefit of the bigger communities, especially the individual churches. And, as we said at the end of the last synod, they will be a hope for the universal Church to the extent:*

58.6 *— That they seek their nourishment in the word of God and do not allow themselves to be ensnared by political polarization or fashionable ideologies, which are all to exploit their immense human potential;*

58.7 *— That they avoid the ever present temptation of systematic protest and a hyper-critical attitude, under the pretext of authenticity and a spirit of collaboration;*

58.8 *— That they remain firmly attached to the local church in which they are inserted, and to the universal Church, thus avoiding the very real danger of becoming isolated within themselves, then of believing themselves to be the only authentic Church of Christ, and hence of condemning the other ecclesial communities;*

58.9 *— That they maintain a sincere communion with the pastors whom the Lord gives to his Church,* *and with the magisterium which the Spirit of Christ has entrusted to these pastors;*

58.10—*That they never look on themselves as the sole beneficiaries or sole agents of evangelization—or even the only depositaries of the gospel—but, being aware that the Church is much more vast and diversified, accept the fact that this Church becomes incarnate in other ways than through themselves;*

58.11—*That they constantly grow in missionary consciousness, fervour, commitment and zeal;*

58.12—*That they show themselves to be universal in all things and never sectarian.*

58.13—*On these conditions, which are certainly demanding but also uplifting, the basic ecclesial communities will correspond to their most fundamental vocation: as hearers of the gospel which is proclaimed to them and privileged beneficiaries of evangelization, they will soon become proclaimers of the gospel themselves.*

PUEBLA

Behind the scenes of the meeting of CELAM in Puebla[5] in 1979, there had been something of a tussle between liberation theologians who wanted to promote the CEBs, and conservative bishops who wanted to circumscribe their freedom. The following passage on basic ecclesial communities is a good example of this tension, as encouragement and discouragement follow one upon the other, and note is taken of both positive and negative passages of *Evangelii Nuntiandi*. Overall the Puebla meeting was felt to be a success, as some positive steps forward—especially on the 'option for the poor'—found their way into the final documents, along with much other material.

The term 'basic ecclesial community' became standard at Puebla, which had not yet been the case at Medellín. This development has been welcomed as an endorsement of the role of the CEB as being

[5] See Appendix 1.

truly the embodiment of the local Church. One reason why the English version has tended to be 'basic Christian community', rather than 'basic ecclesial community', is that the term began to acquire a standard translation after Medellín but before Puebla, before 'ecclesial' became a regular part of both title and theological understanding.

This passage comes from the document on *CEBs, the Parish, and the Local Church*, section 2.1 (629–630).

Basic ecclesial communities

Small communities, especially the CEBs, create more personal interrelations, acceptance of God's word, reexamination of one's life, and reflection on reality in the light of the gospel. They accentuate committed involvement in the family, one's work, the neighbourhood, and the local community. We are happy to single out the multiplication of small communities as an important ecclesial event that is peculiarly ours, and as the 'hope of the Church' (Evangelii Nuntiandi, 58.5). This ecclesial expression is more evident on the periphery of large cities and in the countryside. They are a favourable atmosphere for the rise of new lay-sponsored services. They have done much to spread family catechesis and adult education in the faith, in forms more suitable for the common people.

But not enough attention has been paid to the training of leaders in faith education and Christian directors of intermediate organisms in neighbourhoods, the world of work, and the rural areas. Perhaps that is why not a few members of certain communities, and even entire communities, have been drawn to purely lay institutions or have been turned into ideological radicals, and are now in the process of losing any authentic feel for the Church.

REDEMPTORIS MISSIO

In an encyclical letter on the Church's missionary activity, dated 7 December 1990[6] and titled *Redemptoris Missio*, Pope John Paul II gave words of encouragement to the basic ecclesial communities.

The letter recognizes that the communities, which are small, are a way in which the parish can be decentralized and laity can be aware of playing a more active role through the growth of new ministries. The role of scripture reading and discussion is alluded to, as also is the element of problem-solving and commitment to action. It is recognized that the communities thrive in less privileged areas, and that they are an effective way of spreading the gospel and of laying foundations for a new society.[7] They are imbued with love and are a sign of vitality.

The warnings of Paul VI about remaining in unity with the hierarchy, and about avoiding ideological exploitation, are briefly recalled, but with a somewhat less negative thrust. Overall this passage stands as a recent and very positive endorsement of the theology of basic ecclesial communities, and and at least a theoretical encouragement of their formation in the local churches.

'Ecclesial basic communities' as a force for evangelization

52 *A rapidly growing phenomenon in the young Churches — one sometimes fostered by the Bishops and their Conferences as a pastoral priority — is that of 'ecclesial basic communities' (also known by other names) which are proving to be good centres for Christian formation and missionary outreach. These are groups of Christians who, at the level of the family or in a similarly restricted setting, come together for prayer, Scripture reading, catechesis, and discussion on human and ecclesial problems with a view to a common commitment. These communities are a sign of vitality within the Church, an instrument of formation and evangelization, and a solid starting point for a new society based on a 'civilization of love'.*

[6] But it was not released until 22 January 1991.
[7] For **new society** see Appendix 1.

52.1 *These communities decentralize and organize the parish community, to which they always remain united. They take root in less privileged and rural areas, and become a leaven of Christian life, of care for the poor and neglected, and of commitment to the transformation of society. Within them, the individual Christian experiences community and therefore senses that he or she is playing an active role and is encouraged to share in the common task. Thus, these communities become a means of evangelization and of the initial proclamation of the Gospel, and a source of new ministries. At the same time, by being imbued with Christ's love, they also show how divisions, tribalism and racism can be overcome.*

52.2 *Every community, if it is to be Christian, must be founded on Christ and live in him, as it listens to the word of God, focuses its prayer on the Eucharist, lives in a communion marked by oneness of heart and soul, and shares according to the needs of its members (cf. Acts 2:42–7). As Pope Paul VI recalled, every community must live in union with the particular and the universal Church, in heartfelt communion with the Church's Pastors and the Magisterium, with a commitment to missionary outreach and without yielding to isolationism or ideological exploitation.[8] And the Synod of Bishops stated: 'Because the Church is communion, the new "basic communities", if they truly live in unity with the Church, are a true expression of communion and a means for the construction of a more profound communion. They are thus a cause for great hope for the life of the Church.'[9]*

---

[8] Cf. *Evangelii Nuntiandi*, 58.
[9] Extraordinary Assembly of 1985, *Final Report*, II, C, 6.

Bibliography

Bibliographical details of the books, articles and pamphlets cited in the text are given below. Some of this material is unobtainable in the first world, but a small selection of those books that are reasonably easy to obtain, reasonably easy to understand, and recommended for further reading are marked with an asterisk (*). Some of the material may be obtained from CAFOD, 2 Romero Close, Stockwell Road, London SW9 9TY; CIIR, Unit 3, Canonbury Yard, 190a New North Road, Islington, London N1 7BJ; or Center of Concern, 3700 13th Street NE, Washington, DC 20017.

A more complete bibliography can be found in Guillermo Cook, *The Expectation of the Poor: Latin American Basic Ecclesial Communities in Protestant Perspective* (Orbis, 1985).

A New Way of Being Church: Interviews and Testimonies from Latin America Press (Lima, 1984).

Arrupe, Pedro *see* Dietsch, Jean-Claude.

Azevedo, Marcello deC., SJ, *Basic Ecclesial Communities in Brazil: The Challenge of a New Way of Being Church* (Georgetown University Press, Washington, DC, 1987).

*Barbé, Dominique, *Grace and Power: Base Communities and Nonviolence in Brazil* (Orbis, 1987).

Boff, Clodovis, *Como Trabalhar com o Povo* (Vozes, Petrópolis, 1988).

Boff, Leonardo, *Jesus Christ Liberator: Critical Christology of Our Time* (Orbis, 1978/SPCK, 1979).

*Boff, Leonardo, *Church, Charism and Power: Liberation Theology and the Institutional Church* (Crossroad/SCM, 1985).

*Boff, Leonardo, *Ecclesiogenesis: The Base Communities Reinvent the Church* (Orbis/Collins, 1986).

Catapan, Dom Joel Ivo, SVD, *Sementes de CEBs: Grupos de Reflexão, Oração e Ação* (Edições Loyola, São Paulo, 1989).

Concilium 176: *La Iglesia Popular: Between Fear and Hope* (T. & T. Clark Ltd) (December 1984).

Costigan, Margaret, *You Have the Third World Inside You: An Interview with Paulo Freire* (Workers' Educational Association S.E. Scotland District, 1982).

Cox, Harvey, *The Silencing of Leonardo Boff: The Vatican and the Future of World Christianity* (Meyer Stone Books, 1988/Collins Flame, 1989).

Davies, Brian *see* Walsh, Michael and Brian Davies.

Dietsch, Jean-Claude, *Pedro Arrupe: itinéraire d'un jésuite* (Le Centurion, Paris, 1982).

Eagleson, John and Philip Scharper (eds), *Puebla and Beyond: Documentation and Commentary* (Orbis, 1979).

*Eagleson, John and Sergio Torres (eds), *The Challenge of Basic Christian Communities* (Orbis, 1981).

Fraser, Ian, *Living a Countersign: From Iona to Basic Christian Communities* (Wild Goose Publications, Glasgow, 1990).

Fraser, Margaret and Ian, *Wind and Fire: The Spirit Reshapes the Church in Basic Christian Communities* (Scottish Churches House, Dunblane, 1986).

Fraser, Margaret and Ian, *The Fire Runs* (privately published, no publication date given).

Freire, Paulo, *Pedagogy of the Oppressed* (Continuum, 1970/Penguin, 1972).

Freire, Paulo, *Las Iglesias, la Educación y el proceso de Liberación Humana en la Historia* (La Aurora, Buenos Aires, 1974).

*Galdámez, Pablo, *Faith of a People* (Orbis/CIIR/Dove, 1986).

Girardi, G., B. Forcano, J. M. Vigil, *Nicaragua Trinchera Teológica* (Lóguez Ediciones, Madrid/Centro Valdivieso, Managua, 1987).

Gutiérrez, Gustavo, *A Theology of Liberation* (Orbis/SCM, 1973).

Healey, J., 'Basic Christian Communities: Church-centred or World-centred?', *Missionalia* (Southern African Missiological Society), vol. 14, no. 1 (April 1986).

Hebblethwaite, Margaret in *The Tablet* (16 April, 23 April, 30 April, 7 May 1988; 18 March, 6 May, 5 August 1989) and *Alpha* (17 August 1989).

Hennelly, Alfred T. (ed.), *Liberation Theology: A Documentary History* (Orbis, 1990).

Hoffman, Virginia, *Birthing a Living Church* (Crossroad, 1988).
Kairos Document: A Theological Comment on the Political Crisis in South Africa (1985); available from CAFOD and CIIR.
Kalilombe, Patrick Augustine, *Christ's Church in Lilongwe Today and Tomorrow: Our Diocesan Pastoral Planning Project* (no date given but about 1973).
Marins, José, Teolide M. Trevisan, Carolee Chanona, *¿Salir o quedarse? Compromiso misionero de América Latina en sus 500 años de evangelización* (Centro de Reflexión Teológica Mexico, 1988).
*Marins, José, Teolide M. Trevisan, Carolee Chanona, *The Church from the Roots* (CAFOD, 1989).
Marins, José, Teolide M. Trevisan, Carolee Chanona, *Llegará el dia: las CEBs como propuesta, desafio* (Ediciones Paulinas, 1990).
Maslow, Jonathan Evan, *Bird of Life, Bird of Death* (Simon and Schuster/Penguin, 1986).
Medellín documents: *Second General Conference of Latin American Bishops: The Church in the Present-day Transformation of Latin America in the Light of the Council, II: Conclusions* (Secretariat for Latin America, National Conference of Catholic Bishops, Washington DC, 3rd edition, 1979).
Mendoza, Gabino A. (ed.), *Church of the People: The Basic Christian Community Experience in the Philippines* (Bishops—Businessmen's Conference for Human Development, Manila, 1988).
Mera, Carlos Zarco, 'The Ministry of Co-ordinators in the Popular Christian Community', *Concilium* 176 (December 1984).
Mesters, Carlos, 'The Bible in Christian Communities' in *The Challenge of Basic Christian Communities*, eds Sergio Torres and John Eagleson (Orbis, 1981).
Molina Oliú, Uriel, 'How a People's Christian Community is Structured and how it Functions', *Concilium* 176 (December 1984).
*O'Brien, Niall, *Revolution from the Heart* (OUP, New York/Veritas, 1987).
O'Gorman, Frances, *Base Communities in Brazil: Dynamics of a Journey* (FASE-NUCLAR, Rio de Janeiro, Brazil, 1983).
*O'Halloran, James, *Living Cells: Developing Small Christian Community* (Orbis, 1984; and subsequent revised edition).
Palmés, Carlos in Appendix 3 of *Pro Mundi Vita*, 50 (1974).
*Pitt, James, *Good News to All* (CIIR/CAFOD, 1980).
Plano Pastoral de Conjunto (1962–1965) in *Revista Eclesiástica Brasileira* 17 (1957).
Povo de Deus na América Latina a Caminho da Libertação, 7° Encontro Intereclesial de CEBs, coleção *Fé e Vida*, *CEBs—3* (Edições Loyola, São Paulo, 1988).

Puebla and Beyond: Documentation and Commentary see Eagleson, John and Philip Scharper (Orbis, 1979).

Puebla: Evangelization at Present and in the Future of Latin America. Conclusions (National Conference of Catholic Bishops, Washington/St Paul Publications, 1980).

Rádio do Povo, Rua Santa Cruz, 5 Guaianazes, CEP 08410, São Paulo, Brazil.

Ratzinger, Joseph Cardinal, with Vittorio Messori, *The Ratzinger Report* (Ignatius Press/Fowler Wright, 1985).

'Religious Life Among the Poor: Two Accounts from Brazil', *Concilium* 176 (December 1984).

Road to Damascus: Kairos and Conversion (1989); available from CIIR, CAFOD and Center of Concern.

Scharper, Philip, and John Eagleson *see* Eagleson, John and Philip Scharper.

Schipani, Daniel S., *Conscientization and Creativity: Paulo Freire and Christian Education* (University Press of America, 1984).

Tellería, Leonor, 'The Ministry of Co-ordinators in the Popular Christian Community', *Concilium* 176 (December 1984).

Torres, Sergio and John Eagleson *see* Eagleson, John and Sergio Torres.

Vatican Council II: The Conciliar and Post-Conciliar Documents, ed. Austin Flannery (Fowler Wright, 1975; new edition 1981).

Vigil, María López, *Death and Life in Morazán* (CIIR, 1989).

Walsh, Michael and Brian Davies, *Proclaiming Justice and Peace: Documents from John XXIII to John Paul II* (CAFOD/Collins, 1984).

Winter, Michael, *Mission or Maintenance?: A Study in New Pastoral Structure* (Darton, Longman and Todd, 1973).

Woods, Donald, *Biko* (Penguin, 1979).

Index

193